Crescent Color Guide to

HORSES

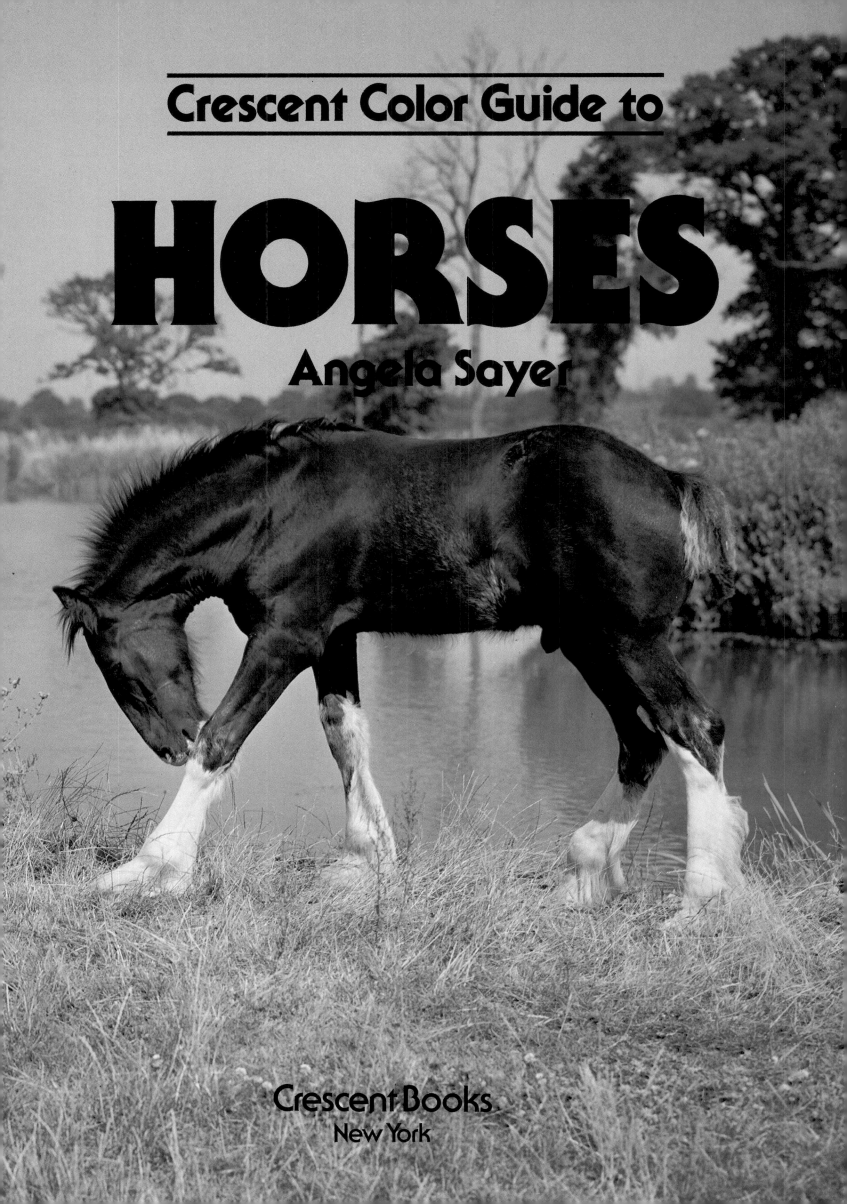

Crescent Color Guide to
HORSES
Angela Sayer

Crescent Books
New York

Copyright © The Hamlyn Publishing Group Limited MCMLXXX

First English edition published by
Deans International Publishing
52-54 Southwark Street, London SE1 1UA
A division of The Hamlyn Publishing Group Limited
London · New York · Sydney · Toronto

ISBN 0-517-31854-7

This edition is published by Crescent Books,
a division of Crown Publishers, Inc.
h g f d c b

Printed in Italy

Photography by Angela Sayer
(Tony Stone Associates: back cover, title spread
and pages 10, 23, 79, 80. Bruce Coleman Ltd—
Hans Reinhard: endpapers.
Bruce Coleman Ltd—David Overcash: page 15 top right.
Bruce Coleman Ltd—J. J. Joly: page 35.
Bruce Coleman Ltd—Peter Loughran: page 77.
Brian Trodd: pages 34 top, 67)

Contents

The History of the Horse

In order to understand the evolution of the horse family, whose fossil record is remarkably complete, it is necessary to imagine conditions on Earth as they were some 50 million years ago in the geological period known as the Eocene. It was during this era that the ancestors of many of today's mammals began to emerge. Conditions were turbulent, and great glaciers and ice fields covered the Earth near the poles, while the rest of the planet's land masses enjoyed tropical conditions. Lush vegetation grew out of the swamps to form areas of forest. The giant reptiles were extinct by this time, leaving niches to be filled by more adaptive life forms.

One of the mammals of the Eocene was a small hare-like creature with slender limbs. It had four long toes on each forefoot, and on each of the hindfeet three long toes. These phalanges enabled the animal to run safely and efficiently over the soft, marshy ground of the tropical forest floor. Its dentition, consisting of very short teeth and a developing system of grinding ridges, was adapted for browsing on the succulent herbage of the palm-like trees, and the thick reeds along the swamp margins.

A Connemara mare with her chestnut foal which shows early signs of becoming grey too.

Shy and nervous and possessing rapid reflexes, this tiny herbivorous mammal was acutely aware of all the dangers in its immediate environment, and was ready to flee at any hint of trouble. Its conformation enabled it to spring away in order to escape capture by the large predators of those times. This small mammal was well adapted for its day, and flourished. Being very fertile, its numbers progressively increased and it showed a growing preference for living in small groups rather than as an individual.

Some thirteen species of this genus have been discovered, ranging in comparative size from a cat to a medium-sized terrier dog. The common ancestor of all the modern horses, *Eohippus*, is often called the 'dawn horse'.

Some of the 'wild' white horses of southern France's Camargue region.

From the eventual demise of the dawn horse until the emergence of *Equus*, the horse of today, over two hundred and sixty intermediate species have been identified and named, which trace the very gradual evolutionary processes that took place during the time span of those 50 million mutable years. As the climatic conditions slowly changed over the next 20 million years or so, the swampy land became dry and great areas of savanna arose. Through the Oligocene 38 million years ago, and into the Miocene period, about 25 million years ago, *Eohippus* also changed in many ways, emerging as *Mesohippus* – larger, with a longer neck and a firmer, more muscular body. This little ungulate's longer legs ended in three usable toes, and its teeth were further modified to pull at the newly evolved grasses.

By the end of the Miocene era, further adaptation had produced the *Merychippus*, the size of a large dog and with a pony-shaped skull. Its teeth were quite different from those of its early ancestors, as a cement-like filling had evolved, making them better for grinding than for chewing, and indicating its role as a grazer, rather than a browser. Although *Merychippus* retained three long toes on each foot, only the central one was actually used in running. This toe was greatly enlarged and strongly hoofed, well suited to the firm ground over which these animals ranged in large herds.

By the beginning of the Pliocene, about 10 million years ago, the first bands of monodactyl horses galloped freely across the vast open plains of their birth. About ten hands high, *Pliohippus* was but one small evolutionary step away from the development of *Equus*, which was to emerge finally at the start of the Pleistocene, a mere million or so years ago. The Earth was then taking on its present landscape and the climate was largely controlled by succeeding ice ages, speeding the development of adaptive species. *Equus* was about twelve hands high, sturdy, swift, fertile and able to withstand extremes of climate: now transformed through the long ages from a furtive forest-dwelling browser to a spirited grazer, the true horse was born.

Herds of wild horses were widespread in Asia and Europe during pre-historic times and one small horse, isolated for centuries in the Great Gobi Desert, has remained virtually unchanged to the present day. This is the MONGOLIAN WILD HORSE or POLJAKOFF, discovered during 1881 in the Kobdo district of Western Mongolia by Russian explorer Colonel N.M. Przewalski who gave it the designation *Equus caballus przewalskii*. The vast tracts of the desert on the Mongolian plateau have proved ideal for the unimpaired continuation of evolutionary processes, and many interesting fossil remains of early mammals have been discovered there. The region is of stony sand, growing water-retaining plants such as saltweed, while clusters of small trees, growing about 10 feet (3 metres) high, form small areas of wood-land. The juicy bark of the trees is browsed by the desert animals and the branches provide shade.

Unfortunately, the discovery of the wild horses brought disaster, for the animals were hunted ruthlessly for sport and food and brought to the point of extinction. The governments of Mongolia and China stepped in and pro-hibited the hunting, and several of the horses were moved to zoos where they could be bred to preserve precious gene pools.

The Mongolian Wild Horse stands from twelve to fourteen hands high and is seen in varying shades of dun, ranging from the palest cream through all the yellow shades to the deeper golden-red tones. A true desert-coloured animal, it has a large, coarse head with short ears and a roman nose which sports an oatmeal-coloured muzzle. The erect mane is dark and matches the rather sparsely furnished tail. Zebra marks are commonly seen on the legs and haunches, and also on the inner side of the thighs. A distinctive dark dorsal stripe runs along the spine from the withers to the tail, and is known as an 'eel-mark'. Horny growths on the inside of the legs, known as 'chestnuts', confirm that the Mongolian Wild Horse or Poljakoff is indeed a true horse.

Great herds of horses are raised by the Mongolian peoples of today, and the modern Mongolian Pony is directly descended from the Poljakoff. Most of

Equus Przewalskii or Mongolian Wild Horse, is dun in colour and has a 'mealy' muzzle and a dark, erect mane.

today's heavy breeds of horses, known as 'cold-blood horses', are thought to have been descended from this root, while the 'hot-bloods' such as the Arabians and the Thoroughbreds, probably came down from another ancient breed, the Tarpan.

It should be noted here that the names 'hot-blood' and 'cold-blood' do not refer to the horses' actual body temperatures, but are terms denoting the amount of Arabian or Thoroughbred blood present in the animal's immediate ancestry.

The TARPAN, *Equus caballus gomelini*– Antonius – survived in the wild state until about 1850, in remote areas of the Ukraine, Poland and Hungary, when it was hunted to extinction as game. A small, shy horse, it was very fast and obviously provided excellent sport for the mounted hunters. The Tarpan evolved during the time when the Great Ice Age forced the northern forest

Equus grevyii, or Grevy's Zebra, the tallest of all the zebras, lives in small herds led by an old and wise stallion. Its behaviour is the same in a zoo environment (*above*) as in the wild (*left*).

horses to the south where they interbred with the plains horses. The Tarpan had a long, pale mouse-coloured coat, dorsal stripe, erect mane and a coarse tail. From its descendants, several zoological parks have started programmes of selective genetically planned breeding, designed to reconstruct the Tarpan in its original form. The Tarpan of today are about thirteen hands high and mouse-dun in colour with the distinctive dorsal stripe very apparent. They often show zebra markings on the forelegs and inner thighs, and when they are subjected to severe winter conditions, they may change their coats to white, like other truly feral animals in similar climes.

HORSES, ASSES and ZEBRAS all combine to form the present day family *Equidae*, and all are monodactyl, although the second and third digits do still exist in vestigial form as thin, tapering splint bones. Very occasionally, these bones bear phalanges and even tiny hooves. Bucephalus, the famous charger regularly ridden into battle by Alexander the Great, is said to have been three-toed.

The largest of the ZEBRAS is *Equus grevyii*, which may stand as high as fifteen hands at the withers. Grévy's zebras live in large herds led by wise old stallions, on the plains of Ethiopia, Somaliland and North Kenya. Their chief enemy is the lion, but they make good use of their keen eyesight and well-developed sense of smell to avoid attack whenever possible. They are able to defend themselves well, using teeth and hooves to great advantage in a fight. The Common Zebra, *Equus burchelli*, is found between Ethiopia and the Orange River in South Africa, and has been divided into subspecies, mainly on the basis of coat pattern distribution, which is very diverse and distinctive.

The Mountain Zebra, *Equus zebra*, formerly inhabited mountain regions in South Africa; its numbers were first severely decimated by hunting, and it now exists only in small groups in special reserves. Its further reduction was caused by the erection of miles of gameproof veterinary fencing which effectively restricted the animal's seasonal movements, and sometimes cut off their access to water in the dry months. The Zebras are closer to the asses than to horses, having long ears, very short stiff manes and tufted tails. They have chestnuts only inside the forelegs, and like *Equus asinus* are native to Africa.

One of the patent-safety mules used by trail-riding tourists down the mile-deep track of Arizona's vast Grand Canyon.

The AFRICAN WILD ASS, *Equus asinus*, differs from the Wild Horse in having long ears, a shorter erect mane, and a tail ending with a mere tuft of hair. Its hooves are narrow and it has chestnuts only on the inside of the forelegs. Its voice is quite different too, as it brays distinctly instead of neighing. Of the two subspecies, the Nubian and the Somali, the latter is often seen to have very distinct striping on the legs. The least horse-like of the asses, *Equus asinus* is most probably the ancestor of today's donkeys.

The ASIATIC WILD ASS, *Equus hemionus*, has five subspecies, all of which are thought to be endangered in the wild, though some are being successfully bred in captivity. The most typical member of the race, known as the Kulan, stands at about thirteen hands high and is a sandy colour, lighter under the body. The ears are smaller than those of the African Ass, and the conformation is generally more horse-like, though the tail is typically asinine. The Persian variety, *Equus hemionus onager*, is somewhat smaller and daintier in build, with a narrow spine stripe which continues to the tip of the tail. Its pale sandy body colouring continues uniformly right down the legs, and this distinguishes it from the other races.

Both the Kulan and the Onager are renowned for their speed and powers of endurance. The foals stand up immediately after birth, and within a few hours can gallop as fast as the adults of their herd. The Onager once provided sport for the members of the nobility who considered its meat to be a great delicacy. The animal's speed and stamina were such that it could not be overtaken by only one horseman, and so it was ridden down by relays of riders, accompanied by packs of hounds. Though legally protected in its native land, the Onager must now verge on extinction in the wild. The Kulan is protected in China and Mongolia by legislation, and it lives in such remote and inaccessible regions that it may well be able to survive successfully in its natural habitat.

Tibet and Sikkim have a comparative abundance of Wild Ass in the form of *Equus hemionus kiang*. The Kiang is a shy animal and lives at an altitude of about 13,000 feet (4,000 m). Although rarely seen, the local people find its dung, which they collect and use as fuel.

All the Equidae can cross-breed successfully, but the various species have different numbers of chromosomes, and so the offspring of most crosses appear as infertile MULES. A true mule is produced only by crossing a female horse, or mare, with a male ass or *jack*, though a horse stallion may be used with a female ass or *jenny* to produce the somewhat smaller *hinny*. The mule is very ass-like, with its long ears, thin legs and narrow hooves, while a hinny looks much more like a little horse. Mules have been used as beasts of burden since Roman times. They are sturdy animals and their tough hides make them less prone to saddle sores and girth galls, than horses used for the same tasks. They have great powers of endurance and can exist for long periods on coarse herbage and very little water, which makes them ideal pack animals, especially in mountain or desert regions.

It was probably between 3000 B.C. and 2000 B.C. that man first began his domestication of the horse family, utilizing three geographically separate species. The people of the Nile valley tamed the African Wild Ass, and trained it as a pack animal, while the Sumerians taught the Asiatic Wild Ass to draw their chariots. The nomadic tribes at first put the asses into service, then they saw the potential of the Mongolian Wild Horses and started to capture, train and breed them, finding them stronger and faster, and ideal as mounts for herding purposes. The Mongolian peoples are natural riders, and soon learned to get the best out of their horses, especially in battle.

From these humble beginnings, horse and man have developed together. No other species has had such a profound effect upon man's culture, and no other animal has so enabled him to achieve his highest aims.

Top: A team of mules prove their usefulness here by pulling a promotional wagon in the annual pre-rodeo parade.

Above: In Spain, donkeys are employed in all types of pack and draught work including sight-seeing trips for the tourists.

11

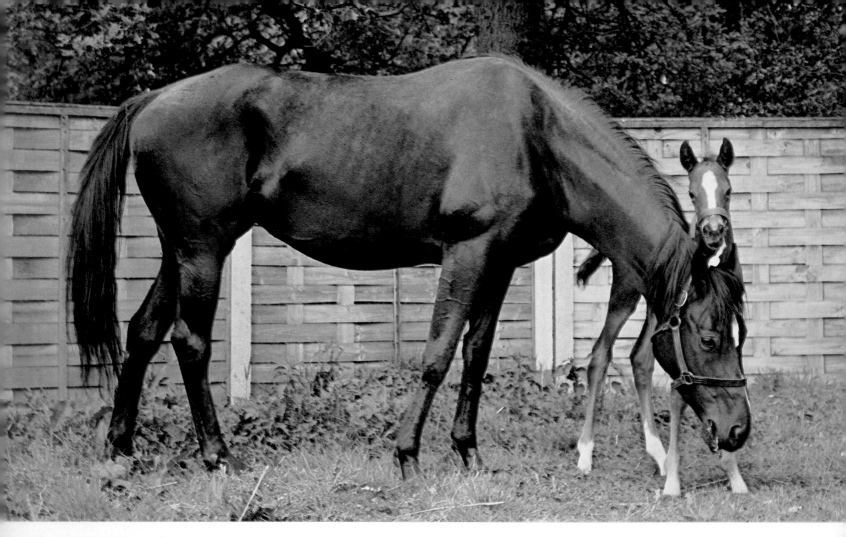

Top: *Invisible Justice*, a black thoroughbred mare grazes peacefully with her petite, light bay Anglo-Arab foal.

Above: This dark chestnut foal has a flaxen mane and tail, white markings on all four legs and an attractive blaze.

COLOUR AND MARKINGS OF THE HORSE

Just as the shape and stature of the horse has changed over the years so has its coloration. From the original dun shade, evolved as the ideal camouflage colour for desert regions, a very few mutations have occurred, and with interbreeding a wide range of acceptable colours is seen today.

GREY is the most dominant coat colour of the horse in terms of the genetic scale, and it heads a series of colours, being followed in diminishing order of dominance by bay, brown, black and chestnut. A grey horse has grey points and a grey mane and tail, produced by an admixture of black and white hairs. It should be of an even shade all over the body. There are lots of variations on the grey theme however: *steel grey* has dark grey or black points; *iron grey* has reddish hairs sprinkled through the coat; a *flea-bitten grey* has tiny spots of dark hairs; a *blue grey* has scattered steel blue hairs. In the *light grey* or *silver grey*, the overall effect is one of total whiteness, and a white mane and tail completes the ethereal effect.

BAY is a reddish-brown, often reaching the hue of polished mahogany. The colour may extend down to the coronets, but it is more usual for the legs to be black, as well as the mane and tail, giving the very smart appearance known as Bay-with-Black-Points. There are varying shades of bay: the *golden bay* is of a yellowish-red tone; the *bright bay* is a lovely glossy tan shade and the *blood bay* a rich bronze.

BROWN horses are recognized by their definite brown muzzles, for their coats may be of any brown shade from one resembling a light bay to one which appears to be jet black. Considered to be one of the smarter colours, brown horses are often selected for use as show hacks or hunters, and like the bay, the brown horse often has black points.

BLACK horses are considered by some to be unreliable, but a true black is a very beautiful animal. The Royal Canadian Mounted Police use only black horses and they certainly present an immaculate and striking appearance when they perform their memorable displays and musical rides. The black has a jet black muzzle and comes complete with black mane and tail. It may have some white present in the form of a star, stripe or blaze, and white leg markings.

CHESTNUT horses vary in shade from the very pale yellowish-red of the *light chestnut* through all tones of reddish-brown to the dark and aptly named *liver chestnut*, which is just the colour of raw liver. Very few horses are uniformly chestnut, most having black or brown manes, tails or points, and some even have very pale flaxen manes and tails. Chestnuts often sport striking white face and leg markings too, which add to their rather showy appearance. The major exception to this rule is the mighty Suffolk Punch, a unique breed of heavy horse which is evenly coloured from head to toe, including the mane and tail, in a decidedly chestnut colour. The Suffolk Horse Society divides chestnut into seven categories for the convenience of its members and for registration purposes. There is *dark chestnut*, a bright liver in colour; *dull dark chestnut*, a dull liver; *light mealy chestnut*; *red chestnut*; *golden chestnut*; *lemon chestnut* and *bright chestnut*.

DUN horses come in a fascinating range of subtle tones and closely resemble the ancient wild horses in having black dorsal stripes or eel-marks. The various shades each have very good descriptive names such as *mouse dun*, *silver dun*, *blue dun* and *yellow dun*.

CREAM is a comparatively rare colour in the horse, and the true creams should have silver manes and tails. This elusive coat colour can be caused by the action of two quite separate genes, one dominant and one recessive, and only test matings can determine which is present.

Horses with coats of softly intermingled colours are given the description of ROAN which is further qualified by the proportions of the variously coloured hairs present in the coat. *Strawberry roan* is made up of red, yellow and white hairs, while *blue roan* has only black, yellow and white. *Chestnut roan* is an admixture of very bright chestnut, yellow and white. A SORREL horse or pony is very similar to a roan, but in this instance there are only two colours in the coat, closely mingled red and black hairs without any white.

COLOURED horses are those which have oddly marked coats of more than one colour. Included in this group is the PIEBALD which has discrete areas of white patching on black, and the SKEWBALD which has bold white patches on any colour other than black. A horse with a coat of two colours plus white is said to be *odd coloured*.

SPOTTED HORSES are comparatively rare and often command high prices. They may be marked in any of several different patterns. The *leopard spotted* has clearly defined dark spots evenly dispersed over a light coat. The *snowflake spotted* has white spots spread over a coloured coat, while the *blanket spotted* is a coloured horse with matching spots only on its lighter coloured rump.

Cave paintings found in France and dating back to 18000 B.C. clearly showed spotted horses, and they were also known to have been in existence in Asia in 3500 B.C. A famous spotted warhorse belonged to the great Persian leader, Rustan, about 400 B.C. and is said to be the ancestor of a long line of Iranian spotted horses. Imported into China by the Emperor Wu Ti about 100 B.C., spotted horses were reverently called the 'Heavenly Horses'. They adorned Chinese art for many centuries and were highly prized by those wealthy enough to own them. Emperor Hsuan T'sung is said to have had a large proportion of spotted horses among the 40,000 animals in his vast and impressive stables.

Perhaps the most famous of all spotted horses is the APPALOOSA, which was originally raised and jealously guarded by the Nez Percé Indians, who developed the breed from horses introduced to the United States by the Spanish *conquistadores*. Today's examples of the breed are often strikingly handsome, and are very unusual in that the black or dark chocolate brown spots can be felt by touch, appearing in bold relief on the fine base coat of the horses.

During the nineteenth century, the owner of the Knabstrup estate in Denmark, acquired a spotted mare, and from her soon produced a similar foal. With careful selection for good traits as well as spotting, the famous Knabstrupper horses were eventually perfected and are renowned for their strength and character. This breed is often chosen for work in the circus ring: they are so striking in appearance and have the added advantage of a perfect temperament for training in liberty work.

A leopard-spotted Appaloosa mare.

Typical Highland pony, mouse-dun and showing an eel-stripe on his spine.

PALOMINO horses are very striking with guinea golden summer coats and flowing white manes and tails. This colour changes with the seasons, the coat growing through pale cream during the winter, and the golden effect being regained with the regrowth of new coat in the spring. A good palomino does not have any dark hairs in the mane and tail nd has a dark skin underlying its golden pelage. This elusive colouring is said to stem from the horses brought to the United States from Spain, where they were originally known as 'Isabella's', having been the favourites in the stables of that Spanish queen.

The MARKINGS found on a horse's head, legs and body have correct and descriptive names. Any small white mark in the region of the horse's forehead is known as a *star*, while a white mark extending down the face, but not spreading beyond the flat frontal region of the nasal bone is called a *stripe*. A white mark which is wider than the frontal bones is called a *blaze*. If the white area extends even further, either onto the cheeks or up over the forehead, then the horse is said to have a *white face*. Occasionally, a small white isolated area is found, usually between the nostrils, and this is called a *snip*.

When we refer to the POINTS of the horse, we mean its lower legs, mane and tail.

Top: The Haflinger is typically bright chestnut and has a light or flaxen mane and tail.

Above: The chestnut pony in the red head-collar has what is known as a 'wall-eye'.

The 'flea-bitten' effect caused by some dark hairs in a grey coat.

A cold, brown pony masked by a covering of icy snow.

WHITE MARKINGS may be present on one, two, three or all four legs of the horse and used to be referred to as *socks* or *stockings*. It is now considered more accurate to refer to these markings quite specifically, describing them as *white to the fetlock*, or *white to the pastern*. In describing body markings, any small areas of unpigmented skin are called *flesh marks*, while small areas of black hairs on a white or coloured coat are known as *black marks*. Small collections of white hairs are known as *flecks*, and a horse or pony may be described as being *heavily flecked* or *lightly flecked*, as the case may be. Larger areas of hair present in the coat, which do not match its general colour are defined as *patches*. Finally we come to the most interesting and intriguing markings of all, those which betray the horse's ancient ancestors. These are the dark stripes which are sometimes found on the legs and inner thighs, and very occasionally on the withers. Known as *zebra marks*, horses with them often have also a *dark dorsal stripe*.

Cranleigh Fredrec is a magnificent bright chestnut Arabian stallion.

Part-bred Arabian colt *Vesta Golden Viking*, a colour called palomino.

Heavy Horses

An unusual German brewery dray, with *Dolly*, a Clydesdale mare, and *Alfie*, a Shire gelding.

In order to develop breeds of larger horses, various laws were passed in Britain through the ages. An example is an act of 1535 which stated that every owner of farmlands over a certain size must keep two mares exceeding thirteen hands in height, to be mated with stallions of at least fourteen hands. Another law, passed later, affected the import of horses, restricting permission to stallions over fourteen hands and to mares of at least fifteen hands. Eventually, the Great Horse of England was developed to carry the great weight of armour-clad knights in battle and for jousting. When firearms were introduced, armour was discarded and lighter horses were required for military use. But towards the end of the eighteenth century, the heavy horses found their niche again, hauling loads by road and drawing the farm implements over the fields.

With the coming of mechanization, it was inevitable that the heavy horses would give way to tractors, but after the novelty of the new machines had passed, it was found that certain types of agricultural work were performed better and more economically by the horse. Horses cope well on heavy clays, where constant use of massive machinery compacts the land and destroys the actual soil structure, eventually reducing the crop yield. Horses can also work in wet conditions where machinery would prove hazardous. On smallholdings and farms, and where there is limited capital, the careful farmer can produce excellent crops for little outlay by using horses to provide muscle power. With costs of energy rocketing, heavy horse power may soon be in even greater demand.

Champions of the heavy horses too are some of the brewery firms of London, who did some careful costings and found that it would be more economical to use teams of such horses, pulling large drays, to deliver barrels of beer to local customers, than using motor transport. The companies not only gain by the cost-effectiveness of using teams of horses, but the eye-catching drays provide mobile advertisements for the various beers as they pass through the heavy traffic of London's congested streets. The brewery teams are very smartly turned-out at all times and the horses are magnificent. Most of the firms enter their teams for competition at shows and they are always enthusiastically received.

London's Hyde Park is the scene of an annual parade of harness horses, and the large, heavy breeds are included. Most of the breweries take part, and other companies bring out their treasured antique horse-drawn vehicles for a yearly airing. Restored antique harness and trappings are used whenever possible, and the parade, which lasts for several hours, is a great attraction for locals and tourists alike.

Various sorts of harness are used on the heavy horses and the art of harness making is still alive and well. For working purposes, the horse wears a padded collar, a saddle pad, and breeching designed specifically for certain implements. The bridle is often decorated, even for everyday work, and for special occasions the horse is decked with brasses.

In olden days, the horse wore brass ornaments carrying magical symbols, in order to ward off the evil eye and to attract good spirits to the fields. It is thought that the first brass ornaments were carried back to England by the Crusaders, taken as souvenirs of battle from the horses of the Saracens, then copied by local craftsmen, each of whom added his own ideas and designs. Well over one thousand different designs were made and many became traditional. Even non-superstitious horse keepers began to add the brasses to their harness, and the star design was a very popular choice. The oldest brasses were made in a beautiful crescent design, and some handmade examples may still be seen on old and treasured trappings. Later, companies had their own designs cast, and for special occasions, commemorative brasses were made, this practice being continued to the present day.

A pair of French Percheron horses, *Tulipe* and *Esperance,* harnessed to a Cornish horsebus.

The horses wear their brasses for decoration and also in the hope of attracting good fortune when they appear in competition, either at shows, or when competing in such events as area ploughing matches arranged by the various Heavy Horse societies and some agricultural associations. Ploughing competitions are generally open to local farmers, smallholders and agricultural workers, and besides offering classes for tractor-drawn ploughs, there are sections for ploughs pulled by horses, always a big attraction. A ploughing match starts early in the morning when the entrants draw lots for plots of land known as 'cants'. Each cant has to be ploughed within three hours of the starting whistle, and the furrows must be of a certain depth and the correct length. Points are allocated for the way in which the first furrow is opened, the general uniformity of the furrows and the quality of the ploughing generally. The final furrow is as important in the points score as the opening one, and the judges spend much time in careful deliberation before making their final placings.

Successful ploughmen or women seem to have an extra rapport with their patient horses, and this becomes obvious at the ends of the cant, when it is essential to lift and turn the plough so that the shares do not spoil the straight line of the previous furrow. The horses move round and turn very gently, one giant hoof at a time, with their soft ears flickering back and forth to catch the quietly spoken commands of their driver. Horse-ploughing is strenuous, but the contestants obviously take great pride in ploughing the perfect cant.

Two fine working Shires about to demonstrate the art of harrowing during England's annual event, the Great Spring Working of Heavy Horses.

Left: Whitbread Brewery's dray drawn by a pair of magnificent grey Shire horses, *Gilbert II* and *Sullivan*. The London brewery firms have done much to promote interest in the breed.

Left: Young's Brewery's *Henry Cooper*, a huge Shire colt, shown in-hand at London's Easter Monday Parade in Hyde Park.

Champion plough-woman Ann Williams competing with *Kelly*, an Irish draught mare, and *William*, a Shire-X-Welsh Cob, working together as a successful team.

Cross-bred horses make exceptionally good animals for farm work and in competitive ploughing. They are often possessed of very steady temperament and respond well to gentle handling and a quiet voice. Most matches have a wide range of competitors, from perfectly matched pairs of Shires to odd couples of cross-breds. In the final reckoning however, it is training and control that win prizes, for no marks are given for good looks. The harness used for ploughing consists of a simple bridle with long lines from the bit to the handler's hands, and a padded collar to which the implement is attached by strong trace chains. Around the horse's girth is worn a simple back band or plough band, which holds up the trace chains at the horse's sides. Sometimes more elaborate trace harness is worn at ploughing matches so that the elaborate brasses and other decorations may be added. Depending on the work to be done and the condition and topography of the land, one, two, three or even more horses may be yoked to the farm implements to be used. Teams of two or three horses may be harnessed abreast or in tandem, or three horses may be yoked Unicorn style with two abreast nearest the implement or wagon, and one well forward and between the others. Farmers often use three horses working in line when they have to initiate a young horse into the discipline of ploughing, yoking it between two experienced horses, so that it has no option but to behave. The heavy horses are generally docile and approach their work willingly. Those who own and work them are their greatest advocates, and it is to be hoped that these gentle giants will go on working for many years.

THE SHIRE was developed in the Midland counties of England, and the first records of the breed in the stud books refer to great black horses of Derbyshire, in the middle of the eighteenth century. The first stallion recorded was born in 1755, a black horse called 'the Packington Blind Horse'. The English Cart Horse Society was formed in 1878 and did much to improve and promote the Shire, then in 1884 its title was changed to the Shire Horse Society. The standard of points for the Shire horse of today requires strength, stamina and power combined with a docile and adaptable nature. Black, brown, bay or grey are all acceptable colours and the height may be from sixteen-and-a-half to seventeen-and-a-half hands. The Shire's head should have a broad forehead between large, prominent eyes. The nostrils should be thin on a slightly roman nose, and the ears long and narrow. A long arched neck sets into deep and oblique shoulders. The back is short and muscular, the chest deep and wide, the quarters broad and strong. Massive legs with square knees end in deep feet and open heels, with fine silky feathers at the fetlocks. In action, the Shire goes straight with a brisk, gay movement. It is a horse ideally suited for its role as a commercial draught animal.

THE CLYDESDALE was the heavy horse of Scotland and northern counties of England and was first bred in the Clyde Valley, being the result of the crossing of several breeds of French and English heavy horses. The Clydesdale Society was formed in 1877 to help protect the breed from being crossed indiscriminately with Shire horses and so losing its unique identity. The Clydesdale was bred to be a very active horse, and was found to be ideal for pulling light delivery vans at a brisk pace around towns, as well as earning high esteem on the land. Many Clydesdales were exported from their homelands to other countries to form the nucleus of breeding studs of heavy horses. The Clydesdale standard requires an average height of sixteen-and-a-half hands, and the most fashionable colour is dark brown, while bay and black are also quite common. Breeders like to see white markings on the face and legs too. The head has a broad forehead between bright, intelligent eyes, the ears are large and the muzzle wide, with large, open nostrils. The massive neck joins slightly oblique shoulders and the withers are high and pronounced. The back is short and the quarters very broad. This horse has large and well-developed hocks and knees, the legs are strong and the feet open and round. Long silky feathering covers the legs from the back of the knee down.

THE SUFFOLK PUNCH probably predates both the Shire and the Clydesdale, and all those in existence today are said to descend from a trotting stallion from Lincolnshire known as Crisp's horse of Ufford. Suffolk Punch horses are always chestnut, all over, although a small white star is occasionally found on the forehead. Manes and tails are of a lighter shade of chestnut than the body. In height this horse stands at about sixteen hands, but is massively built and differs from the two other British breeds in having legs quite free from feathering. The Suffolk Punch was renowned for its ability to pull dead weights, and it was often entered against much larger horses in pulling matches.

THE PERCHERON originated in the Perche region of France and was first bred as a warhorse. It soon proved its worth on the land however, and during the nineteenth century, mares and stallions were taken to the United States and to Britain where they soon became well established. Grey or black in colour, and with a minimum of white, the Percheron is very similar to the Suffolk Punch in conformation but stands a little taller. It is also like the Suffolk in being totally devoid of feathering on the legs. The forehead of the

A Shire mare with her sturdy foal.

Percheron is wide, and the eyes are full with a calm, gentle expression. The ears are medium in size and erect, and the cheeks are deep and curved. A strong, well-balanced neck joins well-sloped shoulders and the back is very short and strong. Huge hindquarters and strong legs add to the powerful overall impression of the Percheon, yet despite its massive build the lines of the head indicate an infusion of early Eastern blood.

Although there are many breeds of heavy horse, one of the best known of the European varieties is the ARDENNES, an ancient breed which developed in the mountainous regions of the Ardennes which intersect the borders of France and Belgium. Mentioned as long ago as 57 B.C. in some dispatches of Julius Caesar, this ancient breed was eventually crossed with Oriental horses to produce a strong and active type of war horse. The French Ardennes is the true representative of the old breed, and is a strikingly handsome horse of either bay, chestnut, roan or sorrel with a dark mane and tail and dark coloured feathering on the legs. Averaging sixteen hands in height, the French Ardennes is strong and muscular with a good action and a very gentle temperament.

The Belgian Ardennes is very similar to the French, but is a little shorter and less stocky, and is considered to be a middle-heavy type.

Many breeds were intermated over the years in order to produce horses with certain characteristics suitable for specific jobs. Some of the heavy horses were crossed with lighter types to increase their speed perhaps, or to make them suitable for riding as well as draught work. In England, when roads were almost non-existent, goods were carried in packs on the backs of strong, surefooted horses. The travelling salesmen who carried their wares around the country in this way were known as 'chapmen', and their horses, Chapmen horses. Later, these were bred in the Cleveland district of Yorkshire, and were chosen as being of a suitable type for pulling the newly-designed coaches in the reign of Elizabeth the First. As carriages became more sophisticated and the roads improved, the Cleveland horses were crossed with Thoroughbred stallions and thus was born the Cleveland Bay as we know it today.

A Belgian draught horse's strength and patience is put to good use pulling a tram in California's fun spot, Disneyland.

A British Royal state landau is drawn by a well-matched pair of Cleveland Bays.

Pedigree Ponies

The author making friends with one of the Hamilton-Renwick Miniature Shetland foals.

All ponies are of the same basic shape, although some are more suited to heavy work, while some are of lighter build and therefore made for riding. The term PONY is applied to varieties of the horse family which do not exceed fifteen hands in height, measured from the ground to the point where the shoulder joins the back, known as the withers. The tiniest of the pedigree ponies is the diminutive SHETLAND while the largest and heaviest breeds are the HIGHLAND and the DALES ponies. The animals ridden in polo matches are always called ponies although these are specially bred horses and often exceed fifteen hands in height.

The pony is not a young horse, for both horses and ponies give birth to foals, the male foal being known as a *colt*, while the female is called a *filly*. A colt becomes a *stallion* at four years of age if he is to be used for breeding, otherwise he is generally castrated as a young colt and is then called a *gelding*. At four years, a filly becomes a *mare*.

The majority of ponies used for general purpose riding and driving are crossbred animals, and are chosen for their size, suitability, colour and temperament. There are also several breeds of pedigree ponies, all of which have very specific standards of points which set out all the requirements for each breed. These standards include such things as the height range, the colours allowed, and the general conformation.

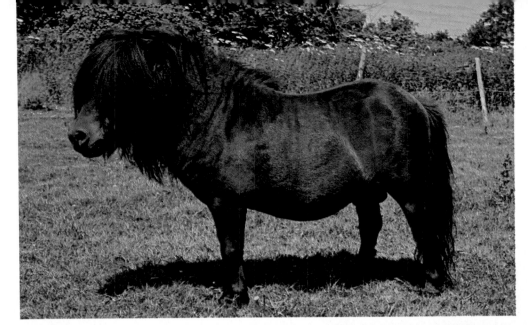

Right: A tiny
Miniature Shetland
stallion.

Below: A roan-
coloured Shetland
mare and her
diminutive month-
old foal.

Gradually, as the islands of the world became populated, agricultural areas were established and transport was necessary to relay goods from the sea inland, and from the farms to the shore. Ponies were often imported and used as transport, and as the years passed so the ponies bred and increased their stock. The isolating effect of such island environments on gene pools caused each island, or island group, to produce its own distinctive pony breed. Some island peoples are very proud of their ponies and prevent the import of any outside stock which might mix with their own, and alter the breed in an undesirable way.

The HAITI PONY is tough and hardy, standing about fourteen hands high. Usually black or brown, it is a useful trek animal, and is in general use today for carrying tourists comfortably on a difficult four-hour trip to historic sites on the island. This rugged breed is said to have descended from the thirty small Spanish horses put ashore on the island by Christopher Colombus in 1493. These unfortunate creatures had spent the three-month journey from Cadiz tied up on the open deck and exposed to cold wind, driving rain and salt spray throughout the voyage.

Off the coast of Nova Scotia, the now uninhabited Sable Island supports several small herds of ponies, said to be descended from ponies taken there by a party of French settlers, early in the eighteenth century.

Two small islands off the Virginian coast of the United States have interesting herds of ponies. The island of ASSATEAGUE is uninhabited, and supports numbers of semi-wild ponies which are gathered in by the herders each summer and driven into the sea to swim across the wide stretch of water to the neighbouring island of CHINCOTEAGUE. This island also has a large pony population, and both herds are separately corralled. All the captured ponies are checked and sorted, and the young stock is separated for the annual auction, after which the breeding animals are allowed to return to the freedom of their grazing lands.

The ponies of Iceland were first brought to the island by the Vikings and were once used for the sport of horse-fighting, and for food. Two distinct types of ICELAND PONY are found today, one used for draught work, which is short, stocky and very hardy, and a fine boned, lighter type used mainly for riding. These ponies have several unusual traits. For example, they seem to have an almost uncanny homing instinct, much more developed than in any other

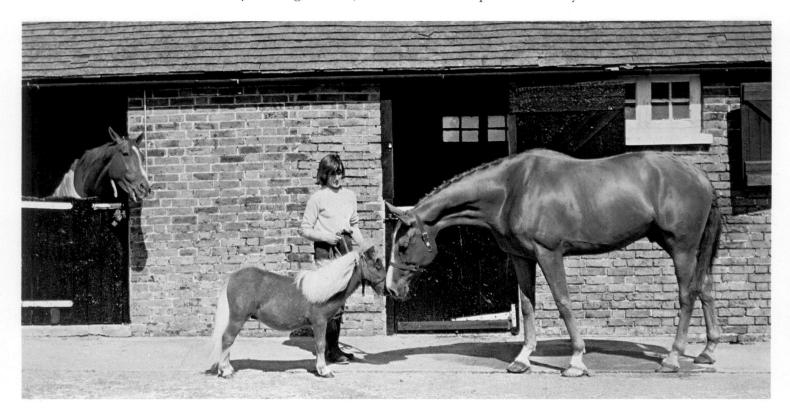

type of horse or pony. Easily trained, they are taught to cover the ground at a fast and very comfortable pace midway between an amble and a trot, and known locally as the *tølt*. Predominantly grey, the Iceland pony is sometimes seen as a dun colour, and very rarely as a dark brown or chestnut, while the FAROE ISLAND PONY is usually brown or chestnut and occasionally black, although they must have stemmed from the same original stock. The Faroe Islands are about 250 miles (400 km) south-east of Iceland and were also visited by the Vikings. In type and conformation both island breeds are similar, being twelve to thirteen hands high, strong and with neat heads.

The British Isles have several pony breeds, known and loved the world over. The smallest is the SHETLAND PONY which developed in the Shetland Islands, north-east of Scotland. Its small size is the product of years of harsh conditions and an extremely inhospitable environment, for when shelter is limited and food is scarce, a small animal is at an advantage; it needs less forage, and its small body area loses very little heat. Bred today as a pedigree pony and in great demand as a child's riding pony or pet, and for work in harness, the Shetland may be of any colour. It must not exceed ten hands at three years of age, or ten-and-a-half hands at four years of age. (We have used hands here for convenience, but registered Shetlands are, in fact, measured officially in inches.) A pony of this breed should be well-made with a short back, broad chest and strong quarters. The legs should have good bone and the round, open feet are very tough. The small and well-shaped head has wide-apart, kind and intelligent eyes, and the ears are short and well placed. The neck is short, strong and very muscular, with a pronounced crest in the

Motor Mouse, the Shetland pony, is introduced to his intended stable companion, a tall steeplechaser.

stallion, and grows a thick and luxurious mane. The tail too is long and full, often sweeping the ground, and is set rather low on the rump.

In action, the Shetland steps out freely, and is very strong for its size. These two factors in combination made the breed ideal for work in the pits, and in 1847, at the beginning of the Industrial Revolution in Britain, hundreds of Shetlands were pressed into underground service in the coalmines, and worked willingly until the coming of alternative forms of energy and different technology made them virtually redundant.

The CASPIAN is another tiny breed, which is quite unlike the Shetland Pony, looking much more like a small and very well-proportioned horse. The Caspian's natural home is along the shoreline of the Caspian Sea, and it is known locally as the Pouseki or Mouleki. Pure breeding stock was brought out of Iran in recent years to start small stud farms in the United States, Britain and Bermuda.

It is thought the Caspian may have been the ancestor of the Arabian horse, for it is a breed of great antiquity, sharing with it many Eastern qualities. In action, the Caspian has a long walk and trot, a smooth, easy canter and a fast gallop. It has an enormous jump for its size and takes fences accurately and with obvious enjoyment. The Caspian standard calls for a fine head with a pronounced forehead and a fine muzzle, large and lustrous eyes and very short ears. The neck is arched and the back short and strong. The legs have fine dense bone and end in neat oval hooves, which are so hard that the pony rarely needs to be shod, even when working on rough terrain. Standing only eleven or twelve hands, this pony is usually grey, bay or chestnut.

Two pretty little Caspian foals out enjoying
the warm Spring sunshine.

Cocum Hawkstone,
a superb Connemara
stallion, posing in his
paddock.

One of the most powerful of the pedigree ponies is the huge HIGHLAND,
another very ancient breed descended from those horses of North Asia that
trekked westwards after the last Great Ice Age. Isolated on different islands
off the Scottish coast, three distinctly different types eventually emerged: the
massive Mainland type, the medium-sized Scottish Riding Pony, and the
smaller Barra, which was probably the one most like the original stock. The
Mainland type is the variety generally recognized as the most desired strain,
and is an intelligent, docile pony, strong enough to carry extremely heavy
loads over very rough and difficult going. This breed was once used by
crofters living in remote areas as a general purpose pony on the land, and by
deer hunters in the Highlands, to carry carcases down from the mountains.

The Highland pony comes in a wide range of colours, including some
unusually eye-catching shades of dun, and many have the stamp of their
ancient forebears in the shape of an eel-mark or dark dorsal stripe, sometimes
accompanied by zebra marks on the legs. The fine head of the Highland is
carried well on its strong neck, and the arched crest sports a long, flowing
mane. The short, curved back is offset by a deep chest and strong quarters,
and the legs are short with strong flat bone.

Connaught in Western Ireland produced the versatile CONNEMARA PONY.
This region of marsh, lake and mountain has been the natural home of an
indigenous breed of pony for many years, and it is from this wild stock that
today's pedigree Connemara has emerged. It is thought that wild ponies
existed in Ireland for many years and that their blood-lines were given an
injection of Eastern blood when some horses swam ashore from a Spanish
galleon, shipwrecked off the Irish coast, in 1588. The Connemara of today is
an excellent child's riding pony, with free straight action. It is willing and
easy to school and often makes an excellent jumping and hunting pony. Grey is
the most popular colour, but bay, black, and brown are common, as well as
dun with black points and dorsal stripe. Roans and chestnuts are less
common. With a typically small and well-balanced head, sharply cut ears
and large, expressive eyes, the Connemara has a look of quality, while the
short back and good shoulders and quarters ensure a comfortable ride. In all,
a charming, alert and well-balanced pony, docile and very hardy.

31

Below: A very strikingly spotted pony foal takes his first look at the world.

Bottom: The Dales foal is bold and happy to sprint around the field, stretching her spindly legs.

The impressive DALES PONY was used for many years as a pack animal to carry coal and lead from the mines in the north of England to the Tyneside dockyards. Large droves of ponies, each heavily laden with twin panniers on their backs were allowed to walk freely, being led by mounted men. At a steady walking pace, the ponies averaged about 240 miles (380 km) every week. Eventually the railways took over the transportation business, and the numbers of Dales rapidly declined, although some of the strong ponies were put to work on small farms in the Yorkshire hills. Many Dale ponies were used by the Army in war, mainly for pulling the heavy guns into position, and they were especially valuable, having immense strength in proportion to their size. The Dales pony may be up to fourteen-and-a-half hands in height, and is often jet black in colour, although bay and brown are common and grey is occasionally seen. Built rather like a small carthorse, the docile Dales is as versatile as it is reliable and makes an ideal family ride-and-drive pony.

Another pony with characteristically 'feathered' fetlocks is the FELL. Roman armies, considering the average native ponies of Britain to be too small to pull heavy loads, imported big black Friesian trotters, and some of these eventually crossed with the native Fell pony, influencing today's type. The legs are short and strong with good bone, and as in the Dales, the feet are of exceptionally hard, blue horn. The Fell has a sweet and gentle expression to match its manners, and makes an ideal utility pony for the whole family, comfortable to ride with its free walk, balanced trot, easy canter, fast gallop and aptitude for jumping.

Oldest of the British native ponies is the EXMOOR which was once known as the Celtic pony, having been used in war by Celtic tribes. Harsh conditions of its moorland environment have ensured that only the strong and hardy animals have survived, and over the generations, the breed has developed into one of outstanding stamina. Bay, brown or dun and with smart black points, all true Exmoors have 'mealy' muzzles of a pale oatmeal shade. About twelve-and-a-half hands high, Exmoors make perfect riding ponies, well balanced and having natural symmetry of movement.

Similar in height and colour is the DARTMOOR, another British moorland breed, showing some of the influence of the Eastern blood of Arabian and Barb stallions turned out on the moors by returning Crusaders. The breed was in danger of extinction due to indiscriminate breeding practices, then a stud book was opened in 1899 and breeding programmes were instituted which saved this charming breed. An elegant pony with great presence and character, the Dartmoor is an alert and active ride.

Even a very young
Exmoor foal has the
distinctive 'mealy'
muzzle seen in the
breed.

There are four quite distinct types of Welsh Pony, each with its own characteristics. Section 'A' in the Welsh Stud Book is for the WELSH MOUNTAIN PONY which must not exceed twelve hands. Section 'B' is for the WELSH PONY, not to exceed thirteen-and-a-half hands, while Section 'C' relates to a similar sized WELSH PONY OF COB-TYPE. Section 'D' is devoted to the largest of the group, the WELSH COB, which must be over that height. Whatever size and shape, the Welsh all have one thing in common and that is their delightful temperament. They are also brave and strong ponies, and most of them jump accurately and well.

The Welsh Mountain Pony has the longest recorded history of all the British native breeds, for it was said that Julius Caesar started a stud farm of such ponies on the shores of Lake Bala in North Wales. He used some imported Eastern stallions with native mares from the mountains, and the offspring were in great demand for riding purposes. Welsh Mountain mares may have been used in the very early days of the development of the English Thoroughbred and were certainly used in the production of the high-actioned Hackney and the polo pony. Section 'A' ponies are ideal for children starting to ride in show classes, and also make excellent, well-mannered leading-rein ponies. Section 'B' Welsh provide perfect show ponies for slightly older and larger children. Section 'C' can often be used by the whole family, being strong and versatile, and also generally go well in harness. Showy Section 'D' cob stallions and colts are the delight of the ring spectators when they are trotted out in hand. Their action at this pace is very impressive. Welsh Cobs also make good all round ride-and-drive animals and are excellent for hunting.

The small island of Lundy lies off Britain's Devonshire coast, and some years ago a shipment of New Forest mares was transported to the island to try to establish a breeding herd on its treeless granite plateau. After trying several different stallions, the LUNDY PONY type became established and standardized, and eventually registration was approved by the National Pony Society. The mares are branded with the official Lundy Flag mark, and a letter and number indicating the year and order of their birth. Preferably dun in colour and about thirteen hands high, the Lundy is an extremely tough, hardy pony with amazing jumping ability.

Below: *Santa*, a fine black Welsh Cob, has proved his worth as a perfect all-round, competitive family pony.

Bottom: Some of the Lundy Island Pony mares grazing on the island's high plateau.

Over 90,000 acres of land in Southern England form the area known as the New Forest. It consists of woodlands interspersed with open common-land covered with gorse and heather. Here may be found small herds and groups of the NEW FOREST PONY, living in semi-wild conditions, but each, in fact, having an owner. Every year, a round-up is organized and expert riders on experienced and well-trained local ponies undertake the hazardous task of gathering in the herds, trapping them in wooden corrals. Here they are identified by their brands and tail-marks, and their owners take the opportunity to examine them, dose them for any internal parasites, and to identify and mark any foals which are to remain in the Forest. Other foals and young stock are auctioned off to go mainly as riding ponies for children.

The New Forest pony is of mixed ancestry, due to the diversity of stallions introduced to the Forest over the years, but is basically twelve to fourteen hands in height and may be of any colour, except piebald or skewbald. The head often shows the influence of some Arabian blood, with dark, kind eyes. This is a generally neat and compact pony, with good action produced from the shoulder, very surefooted and a safe, good-natured ride for children.

Always chestnut and sporting a flaxen or light coloured mane and tail, the HAFLINGER is a general purpose pony which originated in the South Tyrol. A small but strong, typical mountain breed, this pony was first bred for pack purposes only, carrying panniers of hay and stacks of timber, and used also to draw sleighs during the winter months. Its surefootedness ensures its safety for trekking and its good action makes it a comfortable ride. Being an average of fourteen hands high, this pony is rapidly gaining in popularity for all-purpose use in the family. Some Arabian ancestry fined down the rather heavy head and added a large and alert dark eye. The neck is short and strong and the back and quarters very powerful. The legs have excellent bone with very strong joints, and the hooves are round and exceptionally hard.

Just as the Haflinger is always chestnut, so the NORWEGIAN FJORD pony is always dun. Various shades are found from the lightest to dark dun, and the

Norwegian Fjord Ponies are dun in colour and have quite distinctive dorsal stripes which continue along the crest.

35

A Norwegian Fjord mare, the perfect ride or drive pony.

ponies all have black points and black dorsal stripes. The mane is erect, just like that of the ancient wild horse, and is of mixed black and silver hairs matching those of the low-set tail, and occasionally, ancient zebra-like markings are seen about the legs. The Fjord is a very strong, sturdy pony of good conformation, and with a pretty concave head and expressive dark eyes. About fourteen hands in height, this pony gives an impression of great strength. It has a very powerful neck that merges into the shoulder without forming noticeable withers, and the legs are short and hard with feathering on the fetlocks. Although sometimes used for riding purposes, this pony really comes into its own in harness and happily pulls heavy loads over difficult going. With the recent revival of driving as a hobby, many people have opted for the Norwegian Fjord and found it to be the ideal pony for pleasure driving, either on its own, in pairs or in teams. The Fjord has also found favour with trekking centres set up in mountain areas, where it has proved to be a safe and perfect ride.

Working Horses

Of the working horses of the world, it is only the THOROUGHBRED which is involved in racing, the largest single equestrian event of all. Racing in some form is probably as old as horse-riding itself, and there are records of horses racing in Greece around the year 600 B.C. The Ancient Egyptians and the Romans were very fond of dangerous and competitive sports, and both staged mounted races as well as their exciting and often hazardous chariot races. Today, most countries of the world have their horse-racing fraternity, plus an enormous band of ardent punters.

The first recorded flat race in Britain was in 1377 when the young King Richard II, then Prince of Wales, matched his horses against those of the Earl of Arundel. This event took place at Newmarket, later to become the home of horse-racing in Britain. Cromwell put racing on his list of forbidden sports, but it was soon reinstated by Charles II, when it became known as the 'Sport of Kings'. The British Royal Family have always patronized racing. Queen Anne was responsible for the development of the beautiful racecourse at Ascot, so conveniently placed near Windsor Castle in the Berkshire countryside. The first race at 'Royal' Ascot was run in August 1711, the horses each carried 12 stone (75 kg) and raced in heats around the common. The winner was awarded one hundred guineas.

Rafka, an English thoroughbred mare.

Five famous Classic races are held in Britain each year to test the best crop of the three-year-olds. Two of these are held at Newmarket in the Spring; the One Thousand Guineas is for fillies and the Two Thousand Guineas is for colts, and both are run over a course of 1 mile (1.6 km). Two more races are run in the summer at Epsom, over a course of 1½ miles (2.4 km), the Oaks for fillies and the Derby, often called the Blue Riband of the Turf, for colts. In the autumn, the season's final classic race is run over 1¾ miles (2.8 km) at Doncaster, and is called the St Leger. The classic races carry valuable prizes as well as enormous prestige, and the winners are assured of their future as breeding stock.

Other countries have their own famous flat races, and those in the United States are the Kentucky Derby, the Preakness Stakes and the Belmont Stakes, which is the longest of the three, being run over 1½ miles (2.4 km). In France the Grand Prix de Paris and the Prix Royal Oak are held at Longchamp, while the Prix du Jockey Club is held in Chantilly. Only the finest thoroughbred colts and fillies may run in such races, and huge crowds flock to the meetings to back their fancies.

Steeplechasing and Point-to-Point racing developed from the hunting field during the eighteenth century, when keen followers of hounds made private bets as to the prowess of their mounts. The first races must have been quite friendly contests, and one story of such a race describes how a party of horsemen met at the local church and raced across-country to another church, the steeple of which could just be seen across the fields. This was how the first 'steeplechase' was devised.

In 1839, the first Grand National Steeplechase was organized to take place on 26 February, at Liverpool. Fifty-three horses were entered for this much-publicized race, and although it was due to start at 1.00 p.m. the entrants did not start their grand parade until almost 3 o'clock when it was seen that only seventeen horses were to run. There were twenty-nine testing jumps in all, and one horse, Dictator, was killed and others fell, while Lottery, ridden by Jem Mason went on to win. Towards the start of the race the horses had to cross a large field of grass and plough before approaching a strong post and rails, in front of a brook with a much lower landing on the far side. One jockey, Captain Becher, sailed over the rails as his horse fell at this obstacle. He crouched in the brook until the other horses had passed safely, then caught his horse and remounted, little thinking that he would be immortalized by this event, for to this day that particular fence is still known as Becher's Brook.

Ready to be taken to the track is grey *Priory Lad*.

Right: Lester Piggott, a champion British jockey, on one of his countless winners at the Surrey racecourse known as 'lovely Lingfield'.

Above: Many horses train and race in a plain snaffle bit, often with rubber reins to provide the jockey with a good grip in wet conditions.

All Thoroughbreds are able to trace their ancestry to three Arabian stallions – the Darley Arabian, the Godolphin Arabian and the Byerley Turk These great sires were mated with various quality mares, and rigid selection of their offspring was made, using the criteria of speed and stamina. The Thoroughbred horse of today is a living, racing machine. Of the many Thoroughbreds foaled each year, only a small proportion are destined to see a racetrack, for only the fastest of the animals are likely to pay their way in this highly competitive sport. The majority of the colts are gelded and these, with the mares, are usually sold as potential hunters, hacks or polo ponies. Some Thoroughbreds are used for breeding to Arabian stallions in order to produce the most desirable and often very beautiful Anglo-Arab foals, while some Thoroughbred stallions are in demand as sires of hunters and show jumpers.

The English Thoroughbred, carefully bred and correctly raised, is one of the most beautiful horses in the world. It has a refined head and an elegant, arched neck with pronounced withers and a very sloping shoulder. The back is short, the chest deep and the quarters large and muscular, with a well-set tail. The legs are clean and hard, with good bone and pronounced tendons. The Thoroughbred moves with a long striding action, and gives the impression of having unlimited, contained energy.

This breed may be of any colour and may have white markings. The coat is exceptionally fine, allowing muscles and small veins to show clearly, especially after exercise. The height is also very variable. Hyperion, one of the most famous Thoroughbreds of all time, was well under fifteen hands, yet he won the Derby and the St Leger in 1933, as well as several other important races.

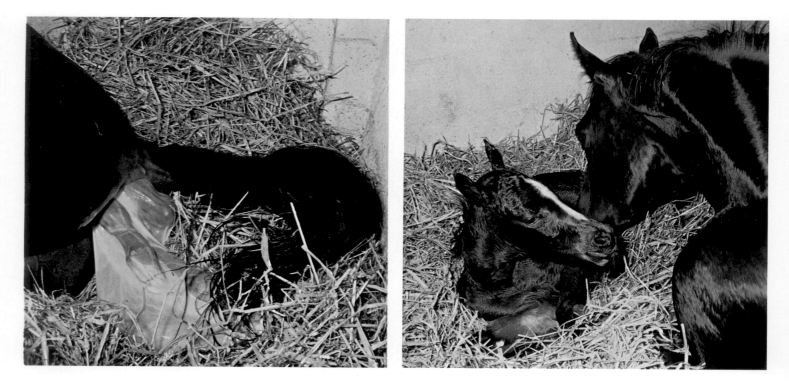

The birth of the foal happens very quickly once the mare goes down. First the forefeet may be seen, followed by the tiny muzzle, then the body slowly emerges enclosed within the amniotic sac.

When Thoroughbred colts retire from racing, the most famous are generally put at stud, and their services offered to suitable mares. A stud farm may have one, or several stallions in the care of a stud groom and his assistants. The stallion is fed on a perfect diet and kept in excellent condition. The stud season starts in mid-February and mares are sent to stay at the stud farm until they are served. Some mares are sent with foals at foot, and some are sent in the final stages of pregnancy. The gestation period in the mare is 340 days, and she usually comes into season a few days after giving birth. The stud offers facilities for foaling-down the mares, so that they are settled and able to be mated during that first season or 'foal-heat'. After a few weeks, and when tests show that the mare is safely in foal, she is transported back home.

Mares have rather uneventful pregnancies and may be exercised carefully to keep them fit and well. When a Thoroughbred mare is due, and the expected foal is likely to be very valuable, it is usual to sit up at night with her, in case of complications during the birth. The signs of an imminent birth are a general restlessness and the formation of a waxlike substance on the udders. Once the mare starts to experience strong labour pains, she gets down and using all her strength expels the foal as quickly as she can. In the wild state, it might be a matter of life and death, for only when she is down is the mare vulnerable to attack. The foal's feet appear first, enclosed within a strong, opaque sac, and one hoof is slightly in advance of the other. As the mare strains, the nose appears, stretched along the forelegs in a diving position. More contractions are needed to push the large shoulders of the foal out into the open air, and then the rest of the body slides fairly easily. The foal struggles and plunges with its forefeet, rupturing the sac, and takes its first shuddering gulp of air, then it can be lifted gently round to its mother's head, where she will nuzzle and lick its face, often making small welcoming, whickering sounds.

After a short rest, the mare raises to her feet and encourages the foal to do the same, pushing and nuzzling it into action. Eventually after two or three false starts, the foal does get onto its ungainly legs and begins to co-ordinate them, and within twenty minutes or so may be searching for the mare's udder in order to feed. This first feed is very important to the foal, as the primary secretions are of a substance called colostrum which contains vital antibodies for the young animal's protection. Once the foal has been seen to feed and the mare has passed the afterbirth, she may take a hot bran mash, and should then be left to rest quietly with her long-awaited baby.

A few hours after birth, the foal is dry with a fluffy coat and is taking an interest in the world around it. The following day if the weather is fine the mare and foal may be allowed out in the paddock for exercise, and by this time the foal will have been fitted with a tiny headcollar called a foal-slip, so that lessons in handling and manners can be started from the beginning.

The mare nuzzles the foal, cleaning and stimulating it, and finally encourages it to stand so that it can take her milk.

As the foal rests in the sunshine the mare watches over her, alert to any danger.

Lactating mares must be fed well, and the foal is taught to feed from a bowl at a very early age. The mare will feed the foal for about six months, but the foal will also eat quite well, nibbling grass and enjoying its ration of corn. Proper programmes of vaccination and parasite control must be carried out after consultation with the veterinary surgeon, otherwise the summer is a time to enjoy watching the youngster grow and develop into a little horse. The foal needs a lot of quiet, firm handling from birth to ensure that it does not learn any bad habits or tricks, for a well-handled foal is easier to break-in and school when older. When the blacksmith calls, he should be asked to examine the foal's feet, and this helps to build a good relationship between him and the young horse. The foal should be brushed all over quite regularly, and if it can be taught to have rugs and towels placed over its back without becoming upset, valuable first lessons will have been learned.

The HUNTER is a horse of Thoroughbred type, but of no particular breed, and is generally selected for its performance over the local type of country-side, its temperament and for its ability to carry the particular weight of its rider for long hours over difficult going. A horse with natural intelligence and a sense of self-preservation makes a good hunter, if it can also jump willingly and safely, and gallop on when required to do so. It must be good with hounds and not show any tendency to kick at the pack, or at other horses. A horse with a good front gives a more secure ride, and one with good conformation will probably feel more comfortable at the end of a long day. The show hunter is grouped into three classes according to the weight it is expected to carry: the light-weight, middle-weight and heavy-weight. The animals are judged on their looks, manners and performance in the ring, where the entrants are asked to walk, trot, canter, and then to gallop on. After calling them into the centre, they are examined closely, stripped of their saddles, and finally the judge will ride the horses on his shortlist to see just how each of them goes. The Hunt horses are usually experienced animals of great dignity and know their jobs really well, enjoying their close relationship with hounds and often seeming to anticipate their riders' intentions.

The hunt servants' horses are chosen for courage and ability rather than good looks.

The HACKNEY is bred solely as a harness horse as it is endowed with an exaggerated lift of the knees and hocks at the trot. This unique action, which must be straight and even, has been bred in, by careful selection over the years, and the best Hackneys command very high prices as show-driving horses. This breed can be traced back to the fourteenth century, but its most influential ancestor was the Norfolk Trotter, bred down from the progeny of an Arabian stallion and a big Yorkshire stallion, early in the eighteenth century. Soon the Norfolk Roadster, as it came to be known, was a popular farmer's horse, well up to weight and able to cover considerable distances at a spanking pace. During the nineteenth century, the breed declined, as other forms of transport came into use. Eventually, with the increasing interest in show-driving, and the efforts of the Hackney Horse Society, the breed was revived and is in a healthy position today. The breed's name is probably derived from the Norman-French word *haquenée*, an ambling horse.

The Hackney Horse usually stands a little over fifteen hands, and in addition to its fiery action it is identified by a small and convex head, small ears and large eyes. The thickset neck sets into powerful shoulders, and the withers are low. The back is short and there is not much depth to the chest. The quarters are muscular and the shortish legs have strong knees and hocks. The fine, silky coat is generally dark brown, black, bay or chestnut. When standing still, the Hackney holds its head high, and the hindlegs are stretched back, giving the impression that the horse is on springs, ready to take off. A smaller version of the Hackney Horse is seen in the Hackney Pony, which shares its larger cousin's action, but in conformation is of true pony type. Formerly used for light deliveries by town tradesmen, it is now bred for show and pleasure-driving and also makes an excellent jumping pony.

Any breed of horse or pony may be used for DRIVING so long as it can be trained to harness work. Conformation is obviously important, though, and some types of horse or pony seem better equipped for harness than others. There are many types of horse-drawn vehicles available, and it is important that the right size and weight is selected for the animal. The harness, too, must be in good condition, so that there is no chance of its breaking under stress, and it must perfectly fit the horse or pony so that it will not rub or chafe.

Below: Highland Ponies are ideal for family riding and can double for driving if trained correctly to harness.

Right: A very smart turnout in the parade of Hackney Horses at the South of England Show grounds.

Left: A fine Hackney in the ring. This one is wearing breast harness.

Below: This elegant lady demonstrates well-fitting harness and an immaculate dog-cart.

HACKING is the name given to general riding out along quiet roads or across the countryside. It is a pleasurable pastime whether undertaken alone or with friends, for the world takes on a different aspect from the back of a horse. Care must be taken in riding along roads, no matter how quiet they are, and it is important to ride on the correct side and to keep well in. Some motorists are very inconsiderate, and pass at frightening speeds, so the horse must be well-schooled and traffic-proof. When riding across-country it is important to obey a strict code of practice. Other stock must be allowed to graze in peace, and must not be frightened or disturbed by your presence. All gates must be left exactly as found – shutting a previously open gate might deprive a farmer's stock of access to water, for example, and leaving a gate open, when it was previously closed, could enable stock to escape onto a busy road, with dire consequences. Finally, the land itself should be treated with care.

Ponies patiently waiting to take tourists trekking at Old Tucson in Arizona, U.S.A.

TREKKING is usually undertaken from special equestrian centres which are situated in areas of great scenic beauty and interest, and where it is possible to ride out across-country and through woodland, on a different route each day. Long slow rides without any fear of traffic, and congenial company, are the essence of trekking, and may also be combined with camping-out, picnic lunches and cook-out suppers. The animals used as mounts for trekking are normally locally bred. Sturdy ponies are chosen and their temperament and docility are taken into account, so that even completely inexperienced riders may enjoy a trekking holiday, knowing that they are completely safe. Trekking centres are found all over the world. Sturdy mountain ponies carry intrepid explorers through the beautiful foothills of the great Himalayan range of mountains. Welsh ponies trek through the valleys of Snowdonia, while tough American-bred ponies take ancient trails.

Keen riders have the habit of forming themselves into various groups and societies the world over. Some participate in ordinary riding activities, while others create special interest groups. In Britain there are several clubs which meet regularly and reinact the grand jousting tournaments of medieval England. They fight mock battles on foot and on horseback for their own pleasure, and also provide spectacular crowd-pulling attractions at horse-shows and carnivals. Wearing colourful costumes and armour, and riding brightly-caparisoned horses, knights ride at full tilt towards one another from opposite ends of the arena, each trying to unseat the other by lunging at him with a long lance.

The knights also fight with swords, axes and lethal-looking spiked balls on chains, known as morning-stars. Large and powerful horses are used by the modern-day knights, who often choose horses of the ANDALUSIAN breed for this work. This horse is strong-bodied, with a good front and striking good looks. Its rather fiery appearance belies its kind and gentle temperament, and these traits make it the ideal choice for competing in the mock tournaments.

Horses are used for all manner of events, games and amusements. Above, a member of the Knights of Arkley team demonstrates the ancient art of the joust. Below is a display of Western riding.

Pioneer Arizona, just outside the city of Phoenix, is the site of a reinacted battle of the Civil War, giving pleasure to both visitors to the open-air museum and to the participants.

Battles of a slightly different type are re-enacted by many groups and societies in the United States. Some simulate famous confrontations between pioneers and the native American Indians, some play out each stage in reconstructed scenarios from the American Civil War. Great attention is paid to every detail; and uniforms, equipment, weapons and locations are all accurately replicated, before the action begins. It is difficult to decide just who enjoys such events the most, the participants or the crowds of enthralled spectators. The ponies seem to revel in it all, from the cavalry drill to the final grand charge. Also in costume, but in a more peaceful connotation, the riders who give displays of various styles of riding, provide great enjoyment at shows, rodeos and carnivals. Western Pleasure Riding Classes are also held in countries outside the United States, and provide an opportunity to dress both horse and rider in unfamiliar gear. A horse must be specially schooled for such events however, and the classes are marked on the horse's abilities in the walk, jog, return to walk, lope, then return to walk, reverse, finally repeating the movements on the other rein.

Hercules, the drum horse, leads the Mounted Troop of the Household Cavalry from the Hickstead All-England Jumping Course arena.

Horses are used by most of the police forces of the world, as there seems to be some quality in the horse that has a calming, or maybe an overwhelming effect on those with whom it is confronted, and it is invaluable for use in crowd and traffic control. London's mounted police are to be seen all over the city, and each day they are on duty outside Buckingham Palace while the Guard is changed, as well as taking part in all ceremonial occasions. These horses are cared for by their own policemen, and rider and horse build up a good working relationship. Police horses must have exceptionally calm temperaments, for they might be subjected to frightening noises in the streets, even gunfire or explosions, and it has been known for unruly crowds to toss lighted fireworks under the animals' legs. No matter how they are jostled, harried or pushed, the police horses never kick out. Instead they are trained to lean into the crowd, gently moving sideways and pushing people out of their way with their strong shoulders and hindquarters.

The most famous mounted police force in the world must surely be the Royal Canadian Mounted Police, often called the 'Mounties'. They originally patrolled vast tracts of virtually uninhabited land in Canada, attempting to keep some semblance of peace between the native Indians and the settlers. Mounted on jet black horses, they were an impressive sight, resplendent in their scarlet tunics and distinctive hats. Today, the horses are used only on ceremonial occasions, when they perform their celebrated and now world-famous Musical Ride.

Below: *Richard*, a handsome dappled grey gelding, ready for police duty outside London's Old Scotland Yard.

Right: London's police horses work hard at crowd and traffic control in the capital's busy streets.

Far right: Neatly turned-out members of the Desert Dolls Drill Team at the Brawley Cattle Call rodeo parade.

The American sport of RODEO began during the early days of the cattle industry. Starting in the dusty cow camps out West, it quickly caught the imagination of participants and spectators alike, and soon spread wherever there were wild horses and steers to be ridden, wild calves to be roped and branded, and wild spirited men to carry out those tasks. Some of the first rodeos staged for spectators were said to have been in Santa Fé, New Mexico in 1847, Deer Trail, Colorado in 1869 and Pecos, Texas in 1883. Today's cowboy has changed very little from the cowboy of those times, and still retains his free spirit and the tenacity and athletic ability necessary for this arduous lifestyle. The professional cowboy has one aim in life and that is to make World Champion. To achieve this means entering about one hundred rodeos during the eleven-month season, and to perform consistently well in the arena as well as handling the business side while travelling between meetings. The events in professional rodeo include steer-wrestling, calf-roping, team-roping, bull-riding, bareback bronc-riding and saddle bronc-riding.

Members of the Girls' Rodeo Association compete in the barrel race, which combines skilled horsemanship with a race against the clock. High prices are paid for good barrel-racing horses and the rider works with the animal for long practice sessions until seconds have been knocked off their running time. The race is run in a cloverleaf pattern around three barrels in the arena, the first barrel being taken in one direction and the second and third in the opposite direction. A five-second penalty is added for knocking over a barrel.

An entrant in the Girls' Barrel Race calmly enters the rodeo arena.

54

Right: The saddle bronc-riding event requires a cowboy to stay in the saddle of the bucking horse for a period of eight seconds.

Below: Hands rush to the aid of a horse which has fallen and become trapped in the chute.

Right: Having completed a successful ride the cowboy may use both hands on the reins until he dismounts.

Above: In this exciting event the horse tows a cow-hide and its passenger at speed around arena markers.

Left: Potential cowboys learn their arts in calf-riding contests at a Western horseshow.

An amusing inter-
lude at the rodeo
provided by the
clown and his two
massive Belgian
Ardennes horses.

    The cowboys' horses play an important part in the wrestling and roping events. In steer-wrestling, one rider, the hazer, keeps the steer running straight while the cowboy leaps from his galloping horse, and wrestles the steer to the ground in a movement known as 'bulldogging'. The horse used for calf-roping is vital, for the cowboy rides after a freshly released and running calf, throws his rope around it and in one fluid motion halts the horse, which stops dead and pulls back on the rope. Simultaneously, the cowboy dis- mounts and runs to the calf, upturns it and ties its feet together with a special 'pigging string'. The calf must remained tied for six seconds, and is then released unharmed. In team-roping, two cowboys work together and both rope a running steer, one putting his rope around the horns while the other catches the hind feet. The first cowboy is called the 'header' and the second the 'heeler'. Team ropers' horses are perfectly trained and know exactly what to do in the arena, working as units with their riders. For all these events the cowboys naturally provide their own horses as training and co-ordination are vital.

    The other horses in rodeo are the 'broncs', horses trained to buck from the moment they are released from the holding chutes into the arena. In saddle bronc-riding a special saddle is used, in bareback bronc-riding, the cowboy has only one hand on the rigging. Both contests require the cowboy to stay aboard for eight seconds.

Showing

Horse shows of all kinds are held in many countries of the world, and there are usually several to choose from every week of the show season. The shows may range from the small gymkhana run by a local riding club to the enormous agricultural show lasting for several days. Special permanent showgrounds are in existence, where regular meetings are arranged, and specialist clubs put on their own annual events.

There are several categories in which horses and ponies may be shown, some being limited by height, and judged on conformation and the animal's performance at different paces. There are classes for working ponies too, which include some low jumps. Tiny children may compete by entering the Leading-Rein classes at some shows, and at the other end of the scale, there are classes for Hunters and Hacks, including the Ladies' Sidesaddle classes. Classes are put on specially for particular breeds and colours; there are classes for pure-bred, part-bred and Anglo-Arabs, all the British native ponies, which may be ridden or shown-in-hand, and classes for Appaloosas and Palominos. Some shows are very specialized and might only offer a few different categories, or be limited to one type or breed of horse or pony. The larger shows have very comprehensive schedules and usually attract large entries.

Before starting on a show career, it is advisable to visit shows of all types, taking careful note of what constitutes a winner and where other horses and ponies have failed to reach the final placings. Many books give helpful hints and advice on show riding and ringcraft.

THE SHOW PONY is often produced by crossing one of the native pony mares with a small Thoroughbred stallion, then the refined youngster is carefully reared and later schooled for the show ring. Only ponies of really good quality stand to win in children's riding classes, for these are judged on their conformation as well as their performance. Before entering any horse or pony in a show it should receive some lessons in ringcraft, and be carefully schooled for the class in which it is to compete. Careful attention to feeding and grooming for some weeks before the great day gradually builds up condition, if this is combined with a proper programme of exercise; and any trimming necessary should be done regularly, combined with checks on the state of the animal's shoes.

Before show day arrives, it is important to check the rules to be sure of having the correct dress for the class, to know what is expected of the pony, and if there are any restrictions on the type of tack used. Once the competitors are in the ring, the elusive quality known as 'presence' may be seen in some of the riders and their mounts. It is a combination of quality and a joy in movement, giving a charismatic air to some animals, and even some rather plain horses show well and with an air of presence if they have been carefully schooled, love their work, and enter the ring at an impressive walk. In the ridden classes, the paces are very important, and the walk is the first pace seen by the judge as the animal enters the ring. It should be brisk and gay. The preliminary schooling should have developed a balanced trot and a calm cadenced canter, with smooth transitions between the changes of pace. The competitors ride around the ring at various paces, and the judge gradually selects those that he prefers and asks the steward to call them into the centre of the arena, until all the entrants are in line. The best of these are then asked to give an individual performance, and the final analysis is made, often after having seen all the ponies stripped of their saddles for a thorough check of their conformation. Finally, the rosettes are awarded and clipped to the bridles of the lucky contestants, who may, if they wish, sedately canter a lap of honour around the ring to the sound of applause from the spectators.

Horses that are too young to be ridden, or those with young foals at foot, may be shown IN-HAND, and such classes are generally well filled at the larger horse shows. The entrants are paraded around the ring being led by a leading rein attached to a special in-hand bridle or smart headcollar. The animals parade in a clockwise direction around the judge in the centre of the ring and are led on the right side of their handlers, so that no part of the horse or pony is obscured. A good free-striding walk helps to attract the eye of the judge and one by one the animals are called into line. Each one is examined in turn and the judge will watch carefully while it is led away, turned around and trotted back in a straight line. It is at this stage in the proceedings that the order of the line is changed, some horses being moved up and some relegated to lower placings, until the final order of the judge is determined and the rosettes are awarded.

WORKING PONY classes are ideal for ponies which are not particularly beautiful, but perform willingly and well for their young riders. Marks are awarded for style and manners, and the pony is expected to clear a small course of low, hunting-style jumps, in a safe and surefooted way. After the jumping phase the ponies all enter the ring together and are lined up in order of their jumping marks. They each give an individual show of walk, trot, canter and a brisk gallop, and show the judge how perfectly behaved they are by pulling up easily after this exhilarating pace and coming to a controlled halt.

The idea for working pony classes came from the United States, where there is a pony hunter division in most large shows. Competition is fairly balanced by splitting the class by pony size and the age of the rider. The Nursery Stakes is for ponies under twelve hands, and children of eleven years and under; ponies under thirteen hands have riders up to fourteen years; ponies from thirteen to fourteen hands are ridden by the under-sixteens; and ponies over fourteen hands are ridden by riders up to eighteen years of age.

Some breeds of native ponies are shown in HARNESS CLASSES and special awards may be offered by their own breed societies. Turnout, that is the way in which the pony and the vehicle have been prepared and presented, is all-important in driving classes, and the colour of the vehicle should preferably complement that of the animal. Carriage colours should be fairly subdued, never garish, although palomino and dun ponies look well harnessed to a float or wagonette of light-coloured varnished wood. The heavier breeds of pony look best pulling rustic or sporting vehicles, while finer-boned animals, such as the Hackney horses look better when harnessed to elegant gigs or phaetons. The harness itself should be matched to the vehicles, the smarter ones may have patent leather trappings while the rustic vehicles require brown or black leather. The pony must be perfectly groomed, with special attention to the mane and tail, which may be plaited or left brushed out and flowing. Its hooves should be well-shod and carefully oiled, while any leg markings should be whitened. The driver and groom must be correctly and neatly dressed and a whip is carried, though never used for punishing the pony. The judges inspect the turnout in the ring, and then the vehicles are driven out for a section of road work. Finally, back in the ring again, the final placings are decided.

Left: Showing in-hand is an art which must be mastered in order to give the pony its best chance of winning.

Below left: An interested pony watches the other competitors as it rests after its class.

Below: A very smart turnout at the annual parade of harness horses was *Wiston Rusty Boy*, a Welsh Cob driven to a Trolley.

WORKING HUNTER classes are held at most large shows. These are usually divided into two sections, one for large hunters of over fifteen-and-a-half hands, and the other for small hunters under that size. The horse may look businesslike rather than beautiful, and a small blemish or two will not be held against it in the final analysis. The working hunter should have plenty of substance and good bone, for in this class it is expected to jump six rustic obstacles of the type that might be found in the course of a day's hunting. The horse is not heavily penalized for knocking the top bar off a jump, but if it has a refusal it will score ten penalties. A second refusal scores a further twenty penalties, while a third means elimination. The jumping section accounts for about forty per cent of the total marks allocated in this competition. After the jumping, the horses enter the ring for the show section. The judges look for a free walk on a long rein and an easy, comfortable trot, followed by a controlled canter, returning through the trot, to the walk. All transitions must be made smoothly and the horse must not resist its bit in any way when asked to reduce its speed. In making their final selection, the judges look for a safe adequate jumper, with easy paces, a good ride and impeccable manners.

Larger shows have classes for young hunters to be shown in-hand, and here the judge is looking for stock with the potential to develop into useful hunters at maturity. There are no weight categories in this class and it is often the best

The winner of the class for Hunters shown In-Hand at two years of age, the beautiful bay gelding *About Time*.

grown young horse that wins. The HUNTERS-IN-HAND classes include those for a brood mare and her foal, a mare in-foal, for yearlings, two-year-olds and three-year-olds. The first and second prize winners in those last three classes go on to compete for the title of Champion Hunter-in-Hand. The horses to be entered in these classes are generally kept in all summer and corn fed, being lightly rugged at night to keep the coat down. The result is certainly a blooming horse, but it may well be too fat and this could lead to problems later, when it is time to break and school it. A high protein diet must be counterbalanced with the correct amount of exercise to produce a fit, not fat horse. Shown in-hand the hunter must be meticulously prepared with a gleaming coat and plaited mane and tail, and is shown in a bridle with matching lead rein.

An all-important factor in showing is to have the correct turnout and first impressions are extremely important. If regular grooming routines have been faithfully followed in the weeks preceding the show, the horse should be in good condition. A thorough grooming through should clean the coat and remove the loose, dead hair, then a towel is used to lift off any remaining dust, before the hooves are oiled or blackened. In the heat of summer a good, non-irritant fly repellent should be used to prevent the horse from fidgeting in the ring, and it is quite permissible to spray a little conditioner on the coat, and to add sheen around the eyes with baby oil. If the horse needs washing, it must be done several days before a show otherwise the coat will lack its natural oils and look dull and lifeless, but the mane and tail may be washed on the day prior to the show if required. Trimming of excess hair is an art to be practised, and should be done regularly so that there is never any need to undertake a really long session. Expert trimming can minimize some of a horse's faults and help to accentuate its good points. The saddle and bridle used in the ring must be spotlessly clean and carefully polished, as well as fitting perfectly. The rider's clothing should be correct for the class, fit well and be smart, clean and well-pressed.

Showing off his perfect manners under saddle
is palomino stallion *Carlden Zeus*.

SHOW JUMPING calls for a very skilled rider and a highly schooled, bold and fearless horse or pony. The sport has become very popular, probably due to its television coverage, which has enabled people who would never dream of going to a horse show to become involved. Horses and ponies have natural jumping ability, but the conformation of some enables them to jump higher and more accurately than others. A horse with the correct musculature and good bone might only need some careful training to develop this natural flair into real talent.

The training usually begins over a series of poles which are called *cavalletti*, and exercises at the walk and trot over these poles in both directions encourage the horse to develop the muscles needed for jumping. Small jumps are added to the schooling sessions, and emphasis is placed on care and accuracy at this stage, rather than achieving height. The jumping and schooling sessions should be made enjoyable for the horse, and a youngster should never be overfaced by asking it to jump a high obstacle before it is ready. The jumping lessons should always finish when it has jumped particularly well, so that it goes to rest with a positive memory to fix in its mind. As the young jumping horse progresses, a great variety of obstacles is added to the schooling sessions. The aim is to teach the animal to jump anything and everything, carefully and accurately on command.

The rules for Show Jumping were drawn up and are controlled by the Fedération Équestre Internationale, and are quite simple to understand. Penalties are incurred which are called 'faults', and the horse with the least number of faults wins the contest. In the case of a draw, time may also be taken into consideration, and obviously, the horse with the fastest time then wins. Four faults are given for any obstacle knocked down, whether it is merely a dislodged pole or a completely demolished fence. Whether the horse strikes the fence with its hind feet, its forefeet or any other part of its body, the faults remain the same. Three faults are given for the first refusal at a fence, and six faults for a second refusal. If the horse jibs for a third time, it is automatically disqualified. Circling in front of a fence also counts as a refusal. Faults are collected for the fall of a horse or rider, and if a time limit is set on the round, and exceeded, then time faults may also be added to the score.

There are all types of show-jumping competitions, some for the very experienced and others for novice horses and novice riders. Most famous show jumping riders started in the Junior classes, learned their skills and gained experience, before progressing to major competitions.

EVENTING is a popular equestrian sport, and is a test of the stamina, courage and training of both horse and rider. The horse must be calm and well-schooled in order to undertake a simple but precise dressage test. This is then followed by a cross-country section during which the horse must cover part of a steeplechase course and then negotiate a series of testing cross-country obstacles within a set time. Finally, the horse must prove to be supple, calm and fit enough to clear a fairly severe course of show jumps within an arena. Good event horses are, not surprisingly, quite difficult to acquire, and having found the right horse, it needs constant and rigorous schooling and exercise to maintain its necessary level of fitness and aptitude.

Eventing began as part of military training when the men of mounted regiments were encouraged to train their horses to a high standard. In the early years of the twentieth century, many European countries held military three-day events, and the sport was first included in the Olympic Games of 1912. After the Second World War, eventing was tried out by some civilian riders and one-, two- and three-day events were arranged. After seeing the eventing at the 1948 Olympic Games, the Duke of Beaufort was so impressed that he decided to make his Badminton Park estate in Gloucestershire a permanent eventing ground.

The first three-day event there was held in 1949, and is now world-famous. The meeting draws competing event horses and riders from all countries. This attracts great crowds of interested spectators, especially on cross-country day, when they line the difficult and sometimes treacherous course, especially near the most testing obstacles. Less difficult but still demanding events are staged for children and their ponies, arranged by local branches of the Pony Club. These are good training grounds, teaching the young people the discipline and degree of schooling necessary for completing all three event elements accurately and safely.

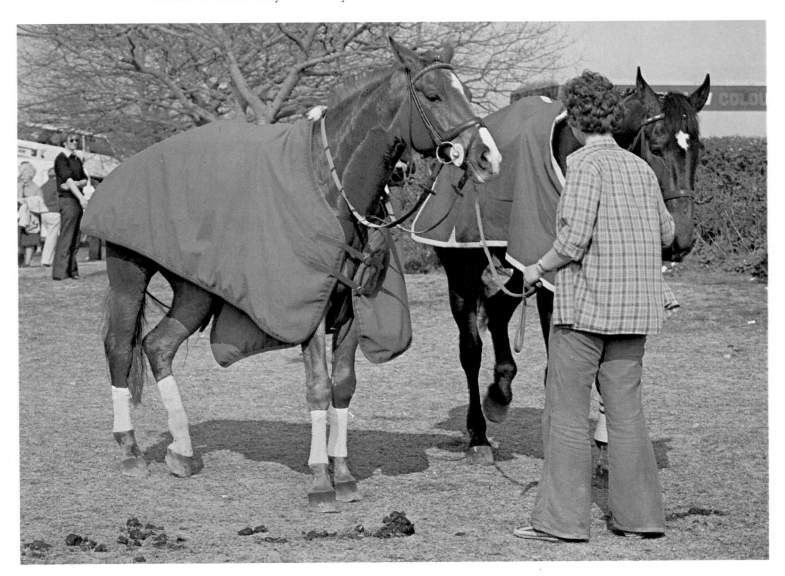

Show-jumpers wait their turn in the collecting ring outside the arena.

ENDURANCE RIDING is a comparatively new competitive sport although the horse has been used in trials of endurance of one kind or another ever since it was pressed into the service of man. In the 1920s, the United States Cavalry started endurance races or competitions, and the sport spread to Canada and Australia, then finally, to Britain. The testing ride is usually over a measured distance of 100 miles (160 km) although Britain's famous Golden Horseshoe Ride is only 75 miles (120 km) long, and is spread over two days. Some of the rides are very gruelling, the Tevis Cup for example, requires horses and riders to cover in one day, 100 miles of the old goldminers' route over the Sierra Nevada, and Australia's 100-mile Quilty Ride in the rugged Blue Mountains of New South Wales must also be completed in one day.

Open to any type of horse, endurance riding attracts quite a selection at the start of a test, all of which must have qualified by completing shorter rides. The rules insist on horses entered being at least fourteen hands high and five years old or more. Rigorous veterinary checks are carried out on all the horses before the start, during the ride and at the finish, and the judging is done in two ways. Awards are given to the rider who finishes in the shortest time, and other awards are presented to the horses which finish in the best physical condition. The veterinary officials have the power to stop any horse from continuing the ride if it does not meet certain criteria at the various check-points. Careful building up of the horse's muscles and performance is carried out for months before the endurance ride is attempted, and the rider must be as fit as the horse. The tack must be very well-fitted and comfortable for both horse and rider. In the Golden Horseshoe Ride it is interesting to note that many Arabian horses win the coveted awards. These small horses, said by many to be the most beautiful in the world, have strength and stamina belied by their rather small stature, fine bone and ethereal looks.

THE ARABIAN HORSE most probably descended from the ancient Tarpan in Libya, North-east Africa or Persia. Similar horses are shown in carvings and drawings dating back almost 5,000 years, some even having details of the

Before the event special studs are screwed into the jumper's shoes to give extra grip.

At the end of the day the competing horses are boxed ready for the journey back home.

animals' names. The Arabs themselves called this breed *Kehilan* which in Arabic means 'thoroughbred' although the horses are divided into many races or strains. The purity of the desert Arabians' bloodlines has always been most jealously and zealously guarded, the introduction of any other breed being unthinkable, and so the Arabian Horse can quite properly claim to be the purest of any equine breed.

The Bedouin took extreme care in breeding their horses, selecting only mares which had proved to have great powers of endurance during long hunting expeditions, or in searching out new trails over difficult and treacherous terrain. The stallions used for breeding were chosen for their intelligence, general conformation and overall beauty.

Today, pure Arabian Horses are bred in stud farms all over the world. These animals are renowned for their qualities of kindness, patience and trust in humans, with whom they often form close attachments. They are alert and have acute hearing plus a good sense of direction. The chief characteristic of the pure-bred Arabian is the beautiful head, with its sharply chiselled lines and the distinctive, concave profile known as a 'dished' face. The eyes are large, round, dark and brilliant, set down in the skull, and the very narrow muzzle has large, flexible and flaring nostrils. Large, wide cheeks and small, sharply-cut and pricked ears all add to lovely lines of the head.

To complete the true Eastern look, the horse has an arched neck and a broad, deep chest. The quarters are broad and level and the back short and strong. The legs have very strong tendons, large hocks and big flat knees, and the pasterns are very flexible. The feet are especially good, being of hard horn, and well-rounded. A flowing mane, and a tail set high on a level with the back, completes the exotic look. Arabians may be found in several basic colours, grey in all its shades is perhaps the most usual, while black is extremely rare. The dark or bright chestnut colours always have a distinct metallic bloom on their very fine coats, which catches and reflects the light.

A New Horse

BUYING A FAMILY HORSE OR PONY needs considerable thought. You will probably keep it for a very long time, and therefore it is important to choose an animal that is suitable for the type of work expected of it. It is best to buy from friends or neighbours whenever possible, so that the pony's history and performance is known to you. The worst way to acquire a horse is from a public auction, unless you are able to check the animal's particulars before the day of the sale. The horse magazines and newspapers run advertisements offering horses and ponies for sale, and there are reputable horse dealers, some specializing in animals for specific purposes. Small children need fairly small ponies, although it is best to start on a pony of about thirteen hands if at all possible, as one of this size will not be outgrown so quickly. A pony for use by the whole family needs to be around fourteen hands high and up to weight, so that it is strong enough to carry the adults. It must be very quiet too, and have a sweet temperament, so that the youngest members of the family may also ride and enjoy themselves without being frightened.

Though looks are not of prime importance in a family riding pony, good conformation does help to make the animal comfortable to ride, while some structural faults may even make a pony dangerous for riding. If a pony has a large, heavy head or a short thick neck it will be permanently unbalanced, while a ewe-neck, which looks as though it is upside-down, causes the pony to hold its head much too high and prevents it stretching and curving its back while jumping. Straight shoulders cause a jerky action at the trot, and give a most uncomfortable ride, and a lack of pronounced withers causes the saddle to slide forward onto the animal's neck. Some ponies have very little space between their front legs; they are then dangerous to ride as their knees and fetlocks brush together in action. The legs are important, and the forelegs should be straight and sound, with sharply defined knees, short, strong cannon bones, sloping pasterns and smooth, well-cared-for hooves. The hindlegs should be well-muscled with good hocks.

It is important to ensure that you have adequate facilities before buying a horse.

68

When choosing the horse or pony its conformation must be checked, also its temperament and health.

BUYING A SHOW HORSE OR PONY is a job for an expert, for then looks and conformation are vitally important. If a native pony is required for show purposes, then it must conform very closely to the standard of points published by the breed society, and must also be registered. It is a good idea to have an expert opinion about any potential purchase, if showing and winning is an important aspect in buying a particular animal. For the ridden Show Pony classes, it is necessary to buy an immaculately schooled pony of the correct height, which looks rather like a miniature thoroughbred, if you are to have any chance of winning. Such ponies are few and far between, and when they are available, will be very expensive. This initial high cost may well be justified however if the pony has already proved its potential by having won consistently, and is sold only as having been outgrown.

Most horses and ponies are bought for general use, and are only entered in small shows for the joy of competing. Having found a possible purchase, you should make arrangements to go and see it, and check it over thoroughly for any defects in conformation. Make sure it has no bad habits, such as biting or kicking and, if possible, see it caught up from the paddock, saddled and bridled, and note its behaviour. Watch the pony being led at the walk and trot, then mount up and try it at various paces to see how well it responds to the aids, and whether or not it is a suitable and comfortable ride. Test whether or not it resists the bit when asked to slow down from a fast pace, and whether it goes forward willingly when urged. Once it is going well, it might be possible to try one or two low jumps before taking it on the road to see how it reacts to traffic.

Right: A grey part-bred Arabian mare with her dark bay colt showing very good conformation and excellent bone.

Right: When first turned out to grass the young foal stays very close to its mother at all times.

Opinion is divided as to whether a mare or a gelding makes the best riding horse. A mare is said to show a more intelligent outlook on life in general, and some mares are very affectionate towards their owners. They do come into breeding season at regular intervals though, and this can cause them to be a little temperamental at those times. Stallions are never used as general purpose riding horses, although some are broken and schooled to be shown under saddle at the larger shows. Colts, destined as riding horses, are usually castrated at about six months of age. They become very tractable and easy to handle, and when they are older, are easily broken-in and schooled for riding. These horses, known as geldings, are usually very amenable if well handled·as youngsters. Several geldings may be turned out together without fighting, or showing the need for establishing a 'peck order', as is the case when groups of mares run out together. One advantage of having a mare though, is that once her riding days are over, she may be used for breeding at least one or two foals.

Left: Looking very fit and well-fed, this Shetland mare is protective of her chestnut foal.

A horse is quite useless unless it has four sound feet, and this fact gave rise to the old adage, 'No hoof – no horse'. Deformities in the feet can cause permanent or intermittent lameness, and faulty shoeing, especially in a young animal, can ruin the feet. The horse's natural foot is beautifully constructed with a round open hoof which can take plenty of weight, spreading the load between the hoof wall, the bars and the frog. The frog itself cushions the foot, acting like a pump as it expands and pushes the heels of the hoof wall outwards.

A badly shod horse develops a cramped narrow hoof, and the frog is prevented from performing its natural functions. Whenever possible, horses should remain unshod, but if used for any roadwork the hoof soon wears down and therefore iron shoes are essential. A good farrier forges the shoes individually to match each of the horse's hooves, checking several times before he is satisfied with the fit. Old layers of dead hoof are pared away and each foot is levelled before the shoes are neatly fixed in place by having special nails driven through the insensitive horn.

Right: The blacksmith or farrier is one of the horse's best friends as good shoeing is very important to all horses and ponies.

Left: When trying a new pony it is a good idea to ask to be allowed to check its reaction to being tacked-up.

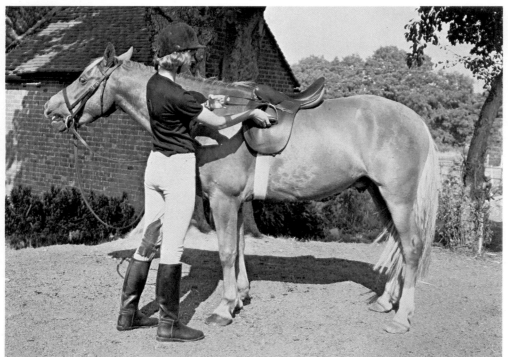

Left: *Shane*, a well-made pony of advanced years, kind, with a keen sense of fun and a perfect schoolmaster.

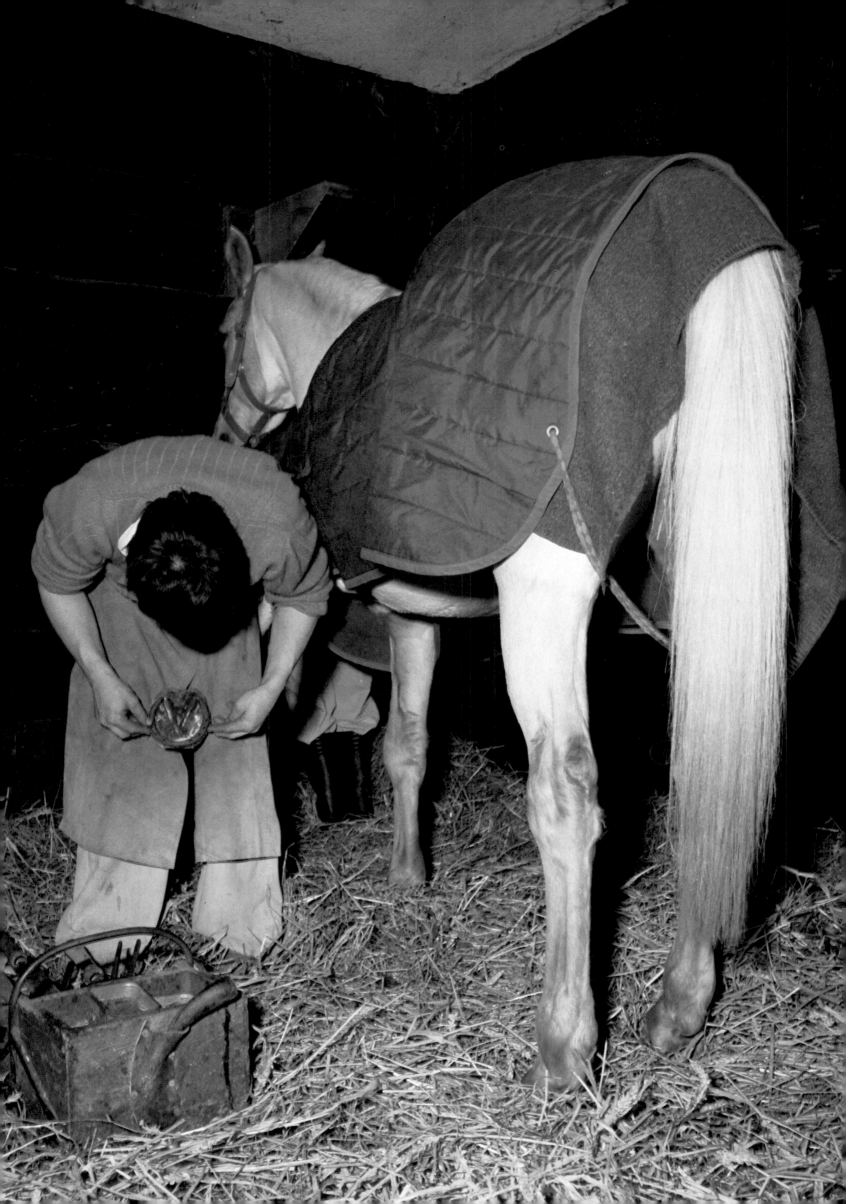

Left: At the veterinary examination the age of the animal is determined by its dentition.

Right: The palomino foal gradually attains a golden summer coat as it grows to maturity.

Having found and tried a suitable horse or pony, it is usual to have it examined by a qualified veterinarian before the deal is completed. Specific rules are laid down for vetting a horse. These entail a full and very thorough examination, the results of which are entered on an official certificate for the purchaser for whom the tests are made, and who pays the veterinary fees. This certificate is known as a 'warranty' and is a form of guarantee of the horse's or pony's health.

The first thing the veterinary surgeon looks for is any sort of vice, such as a tendency to windsuck or crib-bite. He will also note whether the animal is quiet in and out of the loose-box, or shows any sign of biting or kicking at its handler. Next, the teeth are examined with care, for it is by the dentition that the true age of the animal may be determined. A thorough examination of the horse's body is carried out next, and it is checked over from head to toe as the vet feels for any lumps, bumps or other anomalies. The vet listens to the heart and lungs at rest, and then again after the horse has been given some short, sharp exercise. The recovery rate of the heart is also noted, and this indicates the degree of fitness of the animal. If the horse or pony is of a certain breed, or is registered, then special forms must be completed by the veterinary surgeon at this time, which are sent to the breed society, together with a form to be used officially showing change of ownership.

On this form, the vet describes the colour of the horse most accurately, noting any white markings on the head and legs, any flesh marks or other unusual features, such as whorls of hair growth. Any acquired marks must also be noted, and these include such things as bridle and saddle marks, firing and brand marks, scars and tattoos.

One very important part of the veterinary examination is determining the exact height of the horse or pony. To do this, the animal must stand on level ground with all four feet in alignment, and with the head raised to its normal alert position. A special measuring stick is used to check the height from the ground to the highest point of the withers, the height being recorded in 'hands', which are equivalent to four inches. It is possible to obtain a permanent height certificate for ponies over six years of age, and the possession of such a certificate is invaluable when entering height restricted showing and jumping classes.

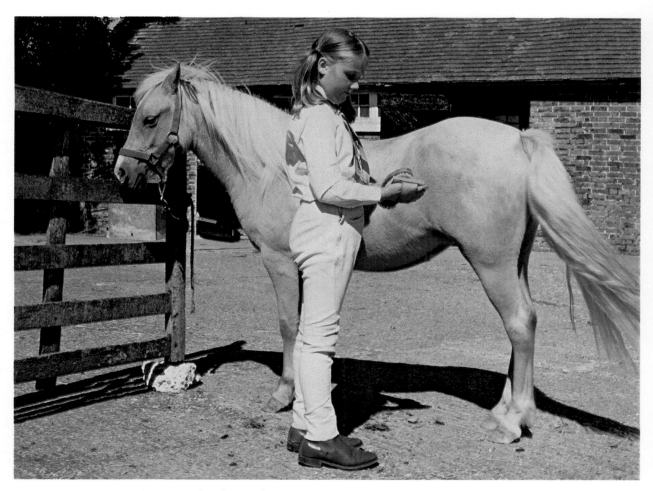

CLUBS AND ASSOCIATIONS exist throughout the world whose main aims are to further interest in horses, ponies and all manner of equestrian sports and pastimes. There are many breed clubs, each of which promotes the correct breeding of a certain type of horse or pony, and works to protect its breed's interests. Other clubs enlist local members to help with running annual shows, and arranging lectures and excursions to studs, stables and shows. Most countries have magazines and periodicals devoted to equine affairs, and these make good starting points for anyone interested in learning more about any horse subject.

For children and young people, the PONY CLUB movement provides a congenial way in which to meet others with similar interests. It is a highly organized institution giving expert help, advice and tuition to its members, as well as publishing excellent handbooks on riding and general horse and pony management. The Pony Club is represented in twenty-two countries, and membership is open to young people up to the age of seventeen years as Ordinary Members, and up to twenty-one years as Associate Members.

Members may, if they wish, attempt a series of proficiency tests, having received expert instruction beforehand. The tests themselves are universally recognized and are conducted by approved and fully qualified examiners. Novices generally start with the confidence-building 'D' Test, which asks simple questions about the most basic aspects of pony care, and requires a demonstration of fundamental riding skills. After this, members gradually work their way up to the general standard of proficiency that is necessary to pass the 'C' Test. This requires a good general standard of riding with a working knowledge of all the basic aids. This test also has questions relating to the correct care of the pony. Test 'B' is more demanding, and is undertaken by more experienced children a year or two after having passed the 'C' Test, and having attended tutorial rallies specially arranged by the Pony Club. The standard of riding required is quite high and a good knowledge of general stable management is expected. The final Test 'A' is very advanced, and those who work hard to pass it have every right to be proud of their achievement.

The pony kept at grass must be fed during the winter.

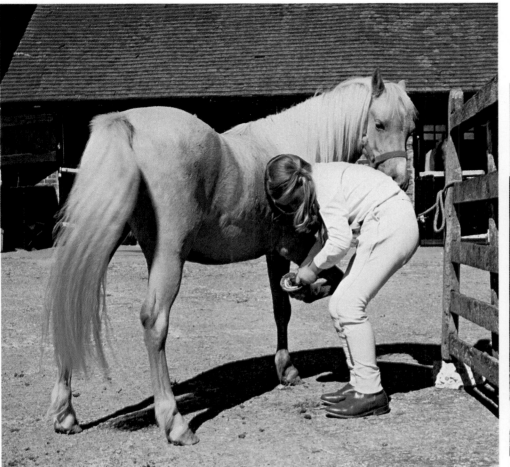

A child will soon learn how to care for her pony by attending rallies arranged by local branches of the Pony Club. Left: Donna cleans the body brush with the curry comb. Right: Using a hoof-pick.

No pressure is put on Pony Club members to take any of the tests, but at the working rallies held by each branch during the school holiday periods, riders are constantly encouraged to improve their general performance and to learn to get the best out of their ponies. Great attention is paid to the correct care and treatment of the ponies, as well as advice and help given on such things as shoeing and the selection, fitting and care of tack. In this way, all the knowledge necessary for passing the various tests is acquired quite naturally and enjoyably. Special events are arranged by most of the Pony Club branches, some of which compete against each other in area and regional games and matches. The mounted games and gymkhanas are always well organized, the emphasis being placed on safety, and all the participants have fun whether they win or lose. Visits to leading horse shows and to stud farms are often arranged, and most branches also hold an annual summer camp, where members can go to stay for one week, taking their ponies. Here they have the excitement of living under canvas or in dormitories, sharing the cooking and chores, spending hours in the saddle, and generally doing all manner of horsy things! After supper and singing around the camp-fire, the members tuck themselves into their cosy sleeping bags for the night, having checked that their ponies are safely tethered and settled.

In the United States, horse riding is a very popular pastime and there are all manner of riding clubs open to new members, each one specializing in its own type of activity. The Pony Club also exists and is well supported. The larger independent clubs arrange excellent teaching sessions in both Western-style and English-style riding techniques, and also put on courses in horse and pony management. Novice adult riders are well advised to join a locally-based riding club, for the functions organized by the committees of these clubs include lectures, seminars, film shows, demonstrations, rallies, meets, and quite often, an annual show. Keen horselovers unable to keep horses of their own can gain a great deal by participating in such club activities, and may well make friends with someone with a spare horse, or someone who will exchange riding facilities for a little help in the stables, with exercise, or with cleaning the tack.

Care must be taken
with mares and
young foals to
prevent them from
getting into hazard-
ous situations.

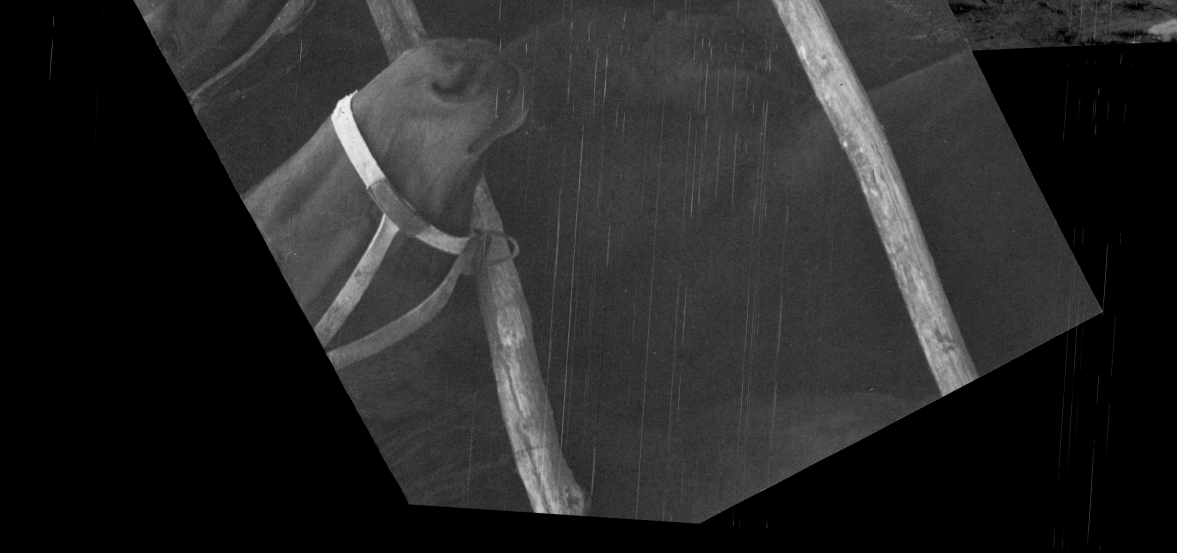

Care must be taken
with mares and
young foals to
prevent them from
getting into hazard-
ous situations.

Training is very important for the young foal before competing in its first show and it should be exposed to new situations.